YOUTUBE MARKETING

The Ultimate Beginners Guide to Learn YouTube Marketing, Tips & Secrets to Growth Hacking Your Channel in 2019-2020

By
David James Miles

TABLE OF CONTENTS

Description I

Introduction.. 2

Features and Impact of YouTube 3

Relations between the Citizens and the Government 14

The Fundamentals of YouTube Advertising.................... 20

Creating A YouTube Account.................................... 25

Using YouTube for Business Purposes......................... 30

Building a YouTube Channel...................................... 33

How Should I Integrate My YouTube Strategies with Other 37

How Income is Generated from YouTube 40

SEO for YouTube 44

Types of Video Contents.. 49

Type of YouTube Videos 56

Putting Together Your Channel 62

Marketing Tools for YouTube.................................... 67

Marketing Your Content... 72

10 Sure Ways to Get More Subscribers........................ 75

Leveraging Your Comment Section............................. 78

Creating Your Ad Campaign...................................... 86

Using AdWords For Video 88

Make Money Through YouTube Sponsorship 93

YouTube Mistakes to Avoid 100

Conclusion 103

DESCRIPTION

Nowadays, people do not just go on YouTube to watch some funny clips of people falling down, cute cats purring, or babies hilariously laughing. It has grown into an extensive platform for the distribution and exchange of valuable information— from make-up tips, cooking to practically anything under the sun.

It offers a variety of channels and videos that provide entertainment, curiosity, amazement and learning.

YouTube is now known to be a great way to be famous and earn money just by making videos from the comfort of your bedroom. Some of today's well-known YouTube personalities became millionaires because of their being successful at establishing and building their channel and fan base, hope that by learning the strategies mentioned in this book, you be able to put them into practice and start working your way up to building your career and hopefully someday, you too could earn a lot of cold hard cash by becoming the next YouTube star! Good luck!

INTRODUCTION

Success on YouTube does not come easy. You will need to work very hard. That is, you must be on the hunt for new ideas and do your best to produce great videos every time. Furthermore, you must not forget to promote your channel. Although you can make money with YouTube, it won't happen overnight. So be patient and don't lose hope.

You must also keep on learning. You may do this by being friends with fellow YouTubers; they may know something you don't. Additionally, the internet provides most of the things you may need to know about YouTube, so make full use of it.

You don't have to wait till you are perfect to become a YouTuber. You will learn the other things you don't know along the way. So get started today. I wish you luck in your quest to making money with YouTube.

CHAPTER 1

FEATURES AND IMPACT OF YOUTUBE

There are several features of YouTube that makes it a suitable platform for video hosting, video watching, and video browsing. Some of the features are listed below:

Playback

When YouTube was initially founded, it required a plug-in called the Adobe Flash Player installed in the browser for viewing on computers. However, in the year 2010, a Beta version of YouTube was created that supported and used the HTML5 standard that was supported by several web browsers due to their multimedia capabilities. This enabled users to watch videos without the Adobe Flash Player plug-in to be installed. The users could now use this new feature and opt for the HTML5 trial. The problem with the Beta version was that only some videos were available. Also, only those web browsers that supported HTML5 using WebM format and H.264 formats could play the videos. In the year 2015, HTML5 became the default playback method for all browsers like Internet Explorer 11, Google Chrome, and Safari 8. An adaptive HTTP-based streaming solution was adapted, which helped to control the quality of videos, and the bit rate of the videos on YouTube through the Dynamic Adaptive Streaming over HTTP. With this success, they are now supported by the Adobe Dynamic Streaming for Flash.

Content Accessibility

YouTube is one of the few video streaming and uploading websites that makes their videos accessible from other web pages. They have a HTML link that is usually below the video that enables sharing. This has spurted the increase in the amount of videos shared on social networking platforms like Facebook and various blogs. In the year 2013, YouTube removed its video response feature that previously allowed users to respond to videos. This was due to the lack of response and use. It is user friendly in a way such that it allows disabling and enabling of comments, ratings, posting of responses, and embedding. Only a few videos can be directly downloaded, like the presidential addresses or weekly reports. These can usually be downloaded as a MP4 file. However, conventionally speaking, it does not allow the download of videos directly. All videos can only be viewed through the interface of its website. With the popularity of videos and the demands of the people for video downloads, several websites, plug-ins, and applications have made downloads of videos easy. A service test was conducted in the year 2009 to allow video downloads for free. There were also test services conducted for download through the payment of a small fee using Google Checkout. With more sites making the download of illegal videos easy, YouTube threatened legal action against several video-downloading platforms to remove their feature enabling downloads from YouTube. However, if videos do not have any copyrighted material, then it is possible to reuse and remake the material without facing adverse consequences.

Platforms

YouTube videos can be viewed through most smart phones and tablets. This can be done by installing the YouTube application for the particular phone or using an optimized browsing page. In the year 2007, using RTSP streaming, YouTube mobile was launched. However, it must be noted that not all videos are viewable on smart phones. Apple enabled YouTube videos on several of its products and this is done by converting the standard YouTube content's transcript and transcode into Apple's default settings of H.264. Today, the videos can be accessed from the iPhone, the Apple TV, iPod Touch, and so on. Due to the complications faced by the mobile version of YouTube, in 2010, YouTube came up with a relaunch of the mobile version. This version operated on HTML5 instead of the Adobe Flash Player. Videos were navigated and controlled using touch screen set up. Android released the YouTube app to enable video watching and video upload.

The YouTube app was initially started in 2012, and it was commemorated by being launched for the iPhone. Apple soon made the YouTube app one of the preloaded apps that came with the iPhone, since the advent of the iOS 6 operating system and the iPhone 5. According to several surveys and data sources, the YouTube app is one of the most widely used apps with about 35 percent of smart phone users using it. In fact, as of 2013, it is the third most widely used app. In 2008, the TiVo service came up enabling the search and play of YouTube videos in the system. It also came up with YouTube for TV, which was customized in accordance to the set top boxes and media devices that had web browsers like Wii video game consoles and PlayStation 3. This was extended in 2009 when YouTube came up with the YouTube XL, which allowed the YouTube web page to be displayed on a standard television screen using a simpler design interface. The YouTube app is also compatible with the XBox Live, and official apps customized for Wii were also created in 2012. This allowed users to watch several videos from the Wii channel. Other such compatible devices include the Wii U and Nintendo 3DS. It is also available on the Roku Player as of 2013. The Wii U Internet Browser uses HTML 5, which is the default code for YouTube; hence videos can be watched and browsed on Wii U. Sony PlayStation 4 has also been compatible with YouTube as of 2014.

Localization

In 2007, the CEO of Google launched the new localization system in Paris. The localized version of YouTube was released in about 79 countries in a standard version worldwide. This used the IP address of the user to switch to the localized version. The YouTube interface identified the territory in which the user was located and customized his or her video viewing experience based on that territory. This is why, in some cases, videos weren't available for all countries. The message, "This video is not available in your country" was displayed on videos with inappropriate content or copyrighted content. About 76 language versions of YouTube are allowed in the interface of the website. Some of them are Bengali, Kazakh, Urdu, Azerbaijani, Laotian, and Burmese; these do not have local channel versions.

Several nations blocked YouTube. For instance, Turkey blocked YouTube from 2008 until 2010, and this was attributed to video postings with offensive material. In 2012, this ban was lifted and a localized version of YouTube was set up under the domain of youtube.com.tr. This was controlled by the Turkish government, and all content was allowed only with the consent and permission of Turkish law. Disputes have also been a common event. In 2009, the British Royalty Agency called PRS for Music about a dispute with YouTube. Music videos were blocked from being accessible to the British population. This came about due to the disagreement in the licensing of major record companies. This was solved in the same year. A similar incident happened to the population of Germany.

Education and Knowledge

According to the curator of TED talks, Chris Anderson, it is possible for the human brain to decode videos. Breaking down videos is easier than breaking down written information or any other form of communication. YouTube revolutionized face-to-face communication, and the fine-tuning of it has made YouTube on par with Gutenberg. Now, YouTube has increased efficiency even more than Gutenberg. This also increased development in science and technology and became a platform for knowledge and learning.

One of the greatest examples of how YouTube revolutionized learning is through the Khan Academy. Salman Khan founded the Khan Academy to teach his cousin. YouTube tutorials were created on various subjects, and soon this became the largest school in the world. With about ten million students, 26,000 videos with 370 million views, YouTube was a mark of how people progressed. It broke down the traditional barriers of learning with decreased costs, uniform content, and reached once inaccessible pockets of the world. Students could now work at their own speed and pace without disrupting their schedule. It resulted in the coming up of technology-forward people who embraced this new knowledge platform. Today, colleges, universities, schools, and other educational institutions make extensive use of YouTube videos to train and develop both teachers and students to create better understanding of their subjects.

Searchable Information

Forrester Research classified YouTube as the largest video platform. In the year 2012, it also happened to be the world's second largest search engine with the only drawback being that search keywords were limited to the video titles, labels, and tags, as opposed to the content of the videos.

Innovation Through Distributed Channels

After YouTube was launched in 2005, the earliest content creators and video uploaders gained massive amounts of views and hits. Their videos had larger viewing audiences, and hence several of them created communities among their video viewers. Chris Anderson stated that people from various areas brought their skills together. These skills were shared, leading to development and challenging people of other geographical locations to develop their skills. This increased innovation and invention. YouTube linked the global world together. For instance, producers of dance companies have noticed that students from America took videos of dance lessons from Japanese dance companies and remade them to suit their style, while Japanese students remixed several American videos to suit their needs. New dance styles, music styles, and new types of cinematography have caused an evolution in videography that is attributed to the global linkage that YouTube provides. Covers and remakes of music videos have served as inspiration to several people, and soon the site became a harbinger of influence, inspiration, and imitation. In fact, a cover by a guitarist received millions of videos and this led to several users creating covers imitating him.

Journalists have found a pattern here; YouTube is not only a platform for watching and hosting videos, but it also became a phenomenon by changing cultures, breaking barriers, and influencing future generations. With this came an influx of inventors. It also provided a platform for scientists, inventors, and researchers to test their theories and concepts. With YouTube, it was easier to collaborate and get answers.

Google purchased YouTube, and after its purchase, several

companies started to dominate the channels. This increased the target audience and revolutionized cultural expression. They were able to receive more hits on their channels, leading to an increase in marketing reach. They also encountered more customer satisfaction and could make their products tailor-made to their customers.

Collaboration and Crowdsourcing

YouTube also served as a way through which people could recognize and form groups and squads. For instance, several projects made use of the video website to assemble people from across the globe to celebrate events. One such prominent case was that of the YouTube Symphony Orchestra which made use of the video website to host auditions. Individuals and musicians were selected based on their performance. This linked people from different towns and failed to discriminate among the various cities and villages. Suddenly, people living in remote locations had the same chance and opportunity as those who were living in larger cities. Mergers were also made wherein people from various locations collaborated to create videos without meeting each other. This broke the geographical barriers of location and time difference. Crowdsourced videos gained massive popularity leading to a large amount of donations. Several non-governmental organizations, charity organizations, and advocates of social welfare created channels to increase their donations. In fact, Lisa Lavie's 57-contributor charity came up with the collaborative video performed by several artists, "We are the World 25 for Haiti." This was done to raise money for the victims of the 2010 Haiti earthquake. Similarly, other charity channels collaborated for giving aid and raising funds for tsunami victims and hurricane victims, among others. "Life in a Day" was a full length YouTube-partnered documentary, which was a collaborative effort of several people, that was the first crowd-sourced movie, released in 2011. It featured 80,000 submitted videos from video uploaders and featured scenes and footage from the life of the video uploaders.

Broadening Awareness of Social Issues

Awareness programs on social issues and help lines were created, leading to more widespread knowledge. Projects like the "It Gets Better" project served as an anti-bullying campaign, which gained massive attention after its launch on YouTube. The project aimed at targeting suicidal LGBT teenagers and discouraging the stigma associated with them. Within a few weeks of its launch, several responses came about from users and celebrities expressing their concern and support. The project gained so much attention that the US President Barack Obama, cabinet secretaries, diplomats, officials, and staff of the government responded positively to this project.

YouTube music videos in support of several causes were also launched. Videos and documentaries relating to the life of people who dealt with bullying, abuse, and other social stigmas were also released. One such was Amanda Todd's video which was titled "My Story: Struggling, Bullying, Suicide, Self-Harm." This was posted a month before her suicide, causing such problems to take the limelight. Media coverage became controversial in this aspect because psychologists believed that the hype and sensationalization of the story would inspire more suicide for the attention. This inspired anti-bullying campaigns, and strategies after bullying were studied and researched in detail.

Many YouTube personalities also used the platform for other good causes. Celebrities and prominent YouTube users used the website to raise money for problems. One such was the Trevor Project that was supported by Tyler Oakley, which raised thousands of dollars for the cause. The Trevor Project advocated the rights of LGBTQ youth and aimed at preventing their abuse and suicide.

Effects on Values and Standards

Entertainment Weekly's "100 Greatest" was a list that featured YouTube in 2009. According to the team there, YouTube was a home for cat videos, cooking shows, celebrity goof ups, and music covers since its inception in 2005. Charlie Bit My Finger was the most watched video as of 2010 and this threw light on the content quality of the videos. Many people in the entertainment industry stated that YouTube had changed the conventional norms of quality. This video served as an example of how the masses responded to video, regardless of the content. The influx of advertising agents and journalists also enhanced the video content on YouTube. The site redefined videos and quality. Several researchers credited the acceptance of low-quality videos, and even ones without mainstream content, to the low expectations of the masses. The lack of professionally made videos did not deter viewers.

Journalism

YouTube also helped to recreate and redefine journalism. The students and researchers of A Pew Research Center studied the effects of YouTube in terms of journalism, and their studies concluded that YouTube had created a new branch of journalism called the video journalism. In this form, eyewitnesses, citizens, and established organizations helped to create content. The most-watched videos were in current affairs or news. Responses and views of the news articles also flooded the scene. This increased flow of information and development of ideas and strategies. YouTube served as a catalyst to increase the response and channel the thinking of the population. News channels also created videos for YouTube propagating and advocating certain news articles that could impact the crowd, and often these channels had more views than the conventional TV views. YouTube also came up with live streaming. The 2012 Summer Olympic Games were covered live on YouTube. Similarly, the site also streamed the speeches of the important political parties during the elections.

It was also particularly useful to bridge gaps in communication. For instance, many news channels could get an idea of the views of the people through comments, ratings, and video responses, which are not something that could be done with conventional forms of journalism.

Direct Effect on World Events

YouTube has been a positive force a well as a catalyst in formulating opinion for the people. One of the videos, "Innocence of Muslims," which was a YouTube video produced in the year 2012, was made by a user in United States, and this was circulated among audiences leading to protests. Several Muslims protested vehemently and believed the entire video to be a mockery of Muhammad. This gained worldwide attention as anti-American violence began to spread, even though the US Government did not advocate the video.

Similarly, a video that showed Neda Agha-Soltan's death gained massive popularity in the positive way. It was captured on a mobile phone camera and depicted the death of an Iranian student during the Iranian election protests in 2009. This gained the George Polk Award in journalism. It became a video that was as important as the news itself. The award meant the acknowledgement of a regular citizen in politics and the role the public played in showing information that could be withheld by journalists. This video also served as a symbol for the opposition movement to the Iranian government.

There were also several videos that triggered issues like the one made by Anwar al-Awlaki. He was an al-Qaeda militant who encouraged attacks against the United States. These videos were eventually removed by the team at YouTube, though in the initial stages, they triggered and inspired violent attacks on Americans. Mockeries, parodies, and documentaries that impacted the public in a bad light were usually removed. One such video was the sentencing of eight video uploaders who uploaded a video that showed the Gangsta culture of teens in the UAE. The video showed mild forms of violence that the court believed showed the UAE in a bad light; this lead to several laws being enacted - one such law being the cyber crime law that stated that severe action would be taken if any act was done to endanger the state. This lead to protests and criticisms, citing right to freedom being curbed. Law enforcement agencies and the government worked with YouTube to avoid malpractice. This was done to remove violent videos by terrorists promoting activities that could influence the viewers. Illegal and dangerous content was removed, and those that proved to be controversial were also removed.

Evolution of YouTube as a Platform for Individuals and Companies

With the advent of YouTube in 2005, it became one of the greatest game changers of the Internet. It was beneficial to video producers, entertainment industrialists, and casting agents. They could now easily find sources of talent. If videos became a mega hit, then producers and agents contacted the video uploader to sign record deals and contracts. Since YouTube's inception, several "YouTube celebrities" have ended up becoming a worldwide phenomena due to their homegrown talent. Many Hollywood companies and record labels have also been on the constant lookout and have partnered with YouTube for this very purpose. Several comedians, bloggers, and singers have been given recognition by celebrities, one notable example being Justin Bieber through Usher. Several celebrities also created channels to increase their fame. Celebrities who were conventionally popular through traditional media also received invitations from the team at YouTube to upload videos, increasing the amount of traffic to the site and growing their target audience and followers to a far greater extent than what they obtained through their TV shows and movies.

In the year 2006, YouTube also partnered with NBC and promoted TV shows aired by NBC. Following this came the purchase of YouTube by Google, for $1.65 billion. This served as a good platform to market products, and advertising companies flocked the scene. Thus, marketing professionals of big companies fled from the television screen to the Internet. Soon YouTube became customer-driven and business-driven. Independent artists, singers, and comedians were able to milk the crowd with little-to-no cost. Four big record labels came into play though they were all very apprehensive given the large amount of copyrighted content that was on the site. YouTube provided a platform to these big record label companies by creating a partnership with them. The lucrative offer was that the site served as a base to make more money for these record labels. In 2009, YouTube partnered with Vivendi and formed Vevo. Vevo was a music service video channel.

YouTube also provided a platform for several channels to increase their profits by investing $875,000 in NextUp, which was a training and tips program for prospective users of YouTube. The company also used celebrities and icons to promote the channel, hoping to get the best of both worlds.

YouTube also was a free platform to test and promote music labels. Videos were categorized as mega, mainstream, and mid sized, which got rave reviews from target audiences. With this, recording artists could test songs before releasing them for free. This increased the amount of hits. YouTube also made its policies very strict as its popularity grew. In 2014, YouTube started to block videos from labels that flouted rules and were not a part of the paid subscription, and they lead to bad reviews and loss of profits.

Video Uploading: Means of Livelihood

In 2007, YouTube launched its very first Partner Program. This was an advertisement revenue-sharing concept that had about 30,000 partners by 2012. Some of the top partners earned about $100,000 annually and others earned much more than just this. Brands that wanted to advertise were to pay the partners money of up to six figures to create and upload ads that would come on their channel.

CHAPTER 2

RELATIONS BETWEEN THE CITIZENS AND THE GOVERNMENT

YouTube has been constantly working to bridge the gap between the citizens of the US and the government. For instance, in the 2007 Presidential debates, people were encouraged to submit questions to the US presidential candidates via a YouTube video. Since visual images prove to be stronger, creating a better impact than mere words, the New York Times journalist Katharine Q. Seelye stated that videos have the power to impact people, and responses in the form of videos can create gusto, influence, and can even shape the way elections are being portrayed. Politics today have been shaped by the Internet, and with video browsing being an available option, candidates are able to channel their views to gain favor among the public. The US Presidential elections are connected with videos, and many presidential candidates have opted to engage the public through YouTube videos. This has enabled the youth to be more actively involved in politics. The youth have also been more participative, and the onset of videos has caused a spurt in the number of voters. The videos have profoundly affected the channel of the elections and have linked the population together with demographic barriers being broken down.

Today, television advertising is still prominent and is still considered an ideal way through which politicians can influence the masses. However, with better resources being channeled towards Internet advertising, more audiences have been reached. The elections saw that only 10 percent of the total budget for advertising was channeled towards the Internet, and it proved to be a grand success. YouTube helped to facilitate communication and engage the public, who were also able to share their thoughts and views and participate actively. Volunteering, funding, financing, and other campaigning formats could be reached due to YouTube. When the public decided to share and give good ratings to the videos, it was more influential as opposed to the advertising done by campaigners. This increased credibility and enhanced public image of the politicians.

Many government entities and important bodies used YouTube as a medium to give out information. Regular news feeds, updates, and important announcements were featured on the channels on the website. In fact, the officially verified YouTube channel of the White House was one of the largest producers of news and dissemination of information to the public. Barack Obama's presidency was a widespread topic to talk about and gained massive YouTube popularity. The impact created by users of YouTube was something that was quite admirable. In fact, politicians became more cautious about what they said, as did journalists and other public speakers. This was done to avoid being mocked or parodied by users.

Today, politicians and celebrities are more accessible than they were in the previous era. Communication from their side is a lot easier, but at the same time, undesirable questions could also be dodged. Videos were created to communicate to the electorate directly. The spontaneity of politics was now gone and replaced by more carefully planned and well-thought-out strategies.

Several government agencies have been actively exploring the ways through which they can use YouTube for their needs. In 2014, a meeting was held with several prominent YouTube celebrities, along with the US President Obama, to find ways through which it was possible to connect with youth. Now, presidents could easily connect with people through videos posted to their channels. The exposure afforded by prominent YouTube celebrities also helped to formulate opinion and gain votes. Social media platforms were also explored and given way to make the Affordable Healthcare Act (ACA or "Obamacare") more accessible. Youth were persuaded and recruited to enroll in ACA health insurance through YouTube videos and spoofs. The President also organized interviews with famous YouTube celebrities to engage the public and to connect with the crowd. Other government entities include water supplying agencies, social welfare agencies, and government programs that list announcements, contests, awareness, and courses to empower the citizens.

Engagement between individuals and private institutions

Educational institutions, private bodies, and firms have found ways to actively engage the audience. Companies create videos to attract the younger generation into joining them, creating a prospective platform to channel resources. These firms have modified their regulations to attract the "YouTube generation." Law firms have played an active role in this. They have created videos to help people to understand and follow the law, to join their firms, and to throw light on what life is like at the firms. The videos have also shown communication from employees and showed how client visits work. Universities have also managed to seek the younger generation through videos. They use this resource as a way to communicate with students and encourage people to apply to the university. These videos are more extensive for they shed light on the various strategies through which people can gain admissions, the criteria colleges look for in applicants, and the campus life, along with publishing question-and-answer sessions. Sample lectures, insights to courses, and information about the college are also common YouTube video topics for universities.

Broadened Expression of Political Ideas

YouTube is an advocate of democracy. This was one of the reasons why it won the George Foster Peabody Award in 2008. It was a place where people could share their opinions, especially in the political domain. Studies done by the Pew Research Center showed that protest was amongst the second most viewed and spoken about topic among video uploaders. This only came second to news and information disseminated by agencies. Protesters have often uploaded videos showing the negative side of a story.

One of the most prominent instances of this is the Arab Spring. In one video, protestors showed injustice done by the political leaders. This created an impact as the ideologies of the protestors gained international recognition. People now use YouTube as a platform to voice their views and plant the seed of truth for the viewers across the world.

This led to the banning of YouTube by several countries. The government agencies of many countries wanted to reduce the exposure of such content to the public, as it tended to cause social unrest and political uprising. Many government bodies also became apprehensive of YouTube. Though this violated the ethics of the people, any video that mocked the national leaders and diplomats was to be taken down. Governments of countries like Syria investigated all the videos pertaining to Syria uploaded on YouTube, and uploaders of videos with faulty content were arrested. Thus, in 2012, to protect the identities of users, YouTube came up with a blur tool which could blur the faces of subjects to avoid identification or recognition.

Those countries that restricted users from certain acts like mockery, parody, and comedy found freedom in YouTube. They could now post videos that were acceptable without getting into trouble. People could also talk about their personal opinion on the government, its agendas, and its policies. Satires about news articles and political parties became a common phenomenon. One such video was the satiric video showing the "Arrest of Vladimir Putin: A Report From the Courtroom," which became a sensation. It was featured on the YouTube homepage for about two weeks.

Through YouTube, politicians and government agencies also are able to channel their viewers into constructive things. Kony 2012, a video featuring the International Criminal Court inductee Joseph Kony, was posted on YouTube causing widespread anger and led to protests favoring the demise of Joseph Kony. The video by Invisible Children, Inc. received about 84 million views in a span of 17 days. This served as an example of how YouTube revolutionized political debate and got the government involved. Subsequently resulting online movements rose up as well.

Benefits of Sharing Personal Information

Several videos came about where users started to be more vocal about their sexual orientation. After the US military's "Don't ask, don't tell" policy, several videos that spoke about the user's opinions and support came about. This was mainly done to spread awareness, increase support, prevent suicide, and create like-mindedness. YouTube developed a way through which people could select their viewers. With this, users could limit how their videos could be watched by people. This mitigated stigma about sharing personal information. Several older generations have also made use of the video platform provided by YouTube to share their life stories. Met with positive views, many videos took a biographical or an autobiographical turn. This broke down barriers, and people were better able to connect with others.

Dangers of Sharing Personal Information

However, there have been videos that have been flagged as inappropriate. These videos include those that contain discussions of a user's self-harm or suicidal tendencies. These tend to have a negative impact on users and can become a form of culture for youth. With YouTube's highly influential ability, such videos can trigger self-harm, suicide, violent behavior, and protests. Regularity of viewing can affect mindsets. Opinionated videos that advocate a certain form of culture can cause humiliation and physical harm. These motivate a one-sided view.

One such video was the beating up of a female cheerleader by teenagers of a school that resulted in the loss of her sight and hearing. Violent videos were always discouraged. These usually gain media attention, and such videos also inspired documentaries by NGOs that advocated the rights of people. There are many cases where popular users have abused their status by manipulating their fans. False accounts and videos have been created, which have altered the mindsets of the fans both emotionally and physically. Many of these go unreported though a few have gained attention. Videos have also triggered suicide, murders, and theft.

Advertising and Marketing

YouTube also has played a pivotal role in advertisement and marketing. It has been able to generate views and hits for small companies who have come to play. Previously, only large companies with enough resources could advertise on the main screen. Today, smaller companies can create channels, track their videos, check their views, promote their products, and appear on the main screen as well. The videos can also feature instructional content on the products that the company is promoting. These videos reduce the amount of resources required to be spent training customers and generate maximum attention towards the product.

The team at YouTube is also constantly trying to revolutionize advertising. By creating similar channels, and grouping products and similar companies together, they are working extensively towards obtaining content and videos easily for the end user.

Measurement of Mainstream Opinion

YouTube also serves as a way by which people's opinion can be measured. Videos usually have a view counter that tells the user how many hits their video has received. Apart from just this, the comments section in the video gives one an idea of how the public responds to the content. In fact, the more views a video gets, the more attention it has attracted. This was specific in the cases of popular cover songs, how-to videos, and so on, wherein celebrities, recording companies, and production houses advocated and promoted those videos. Though several companies acknowledged that one could not gauge the popularity of the videos or the attention span of the target audience, they nonetheless promoted music videos. Video hits weren't necessarily a mark of fanatic attachment, but there were more concrete forms to measure this through sale of CDs and records. However, view count has been a faithful meter to understand the dynamics of the population. Additionally, in order to obtain more sales in concert tickets and promotional merchandise, videos have played a significant role.

In 2013, the YouTube Music Awards were created, which were solely based on the amount of hits that a particular artist received. Thus, it was the public who decided the amounts of votes and the winner instead of judges. It has also known to grow audiences, increase the levels of talent amongst people, and generate bigger revenue for the entertainment industry.

CHAPTER 3

THE FUNDAMENTALS OF YOUTUBE ADVERTISING

Advertising on YouTube is a serious endeavor. If done right, you can generate quite a large number of conversions, build up brand awareness and even help promote your own channel. However, YouTube advertising is no small expense. While the cost of running the ads can vary, there are initial costs associated with creating the YouTube ad itself. However, since a YouTube video ad is essentially a commercial, we won't be covering how to make one. Instead, we'll be discussing how YouTube advertising works, how you can get the most out of your advertising dollar and the different types of YouTube ads available.

AdWords

Since YouTube is owned by Google, you're going to need what's known as a Google AdWords account. AdWords is their advertising system that allows for you to advertise through Google's search engine. Outside of video ads, AdWords is a paid advertising service that will put your website links first after specific searches are made in Google.

Creating an advertising account with Google is fairly simple. Once you do that, you'll need to link your YouTube channel to the account. This will allow for you to select which videos you want to be shown when running an ad.

Ad Types:

YouTube has a few different types of advertisements available for you to utilize. These all have different costs and benefits, depending on what your goals are.

TrueView

TrueView ads are created with both the advertiser and the consumer in mind. There are two different classes of TrueView ads, In-Stream and Video Discovery. A TrueView In-Stream video ad can run for as long as you like, but consumers always have the option to skip after the first five seconds. If the viewer skips before 30 seconds are up, you aren't charged for the ad spot.

The value behind this is that you won't end up boring customers or consumers who aren't interested in your product. And, since you can run your ad for as long as you like, a consumer who is interested in what you have to say will be more than willing to sit and watch the entire thing. This really is a win-win situation when it comes to advertising.

The second type of TrueView ad is known as Video Discovery. Video Discovery simply means that your video is placed in key locations on YouTube, usually at the top of the recommended videos or in the search section. This simply sticks your video up at the top and allows for consumers who are interested to click on it and watch your ad. You are charged, however, every time a viewer clicks on that ad, regardless of how long they watch it.

Unskippable Ads:

If you'd prefer that your viewers see the entirety of your ad, without the option to skip, then you'll need to simply use either the pre-roll or mid-roll ad option. Pre-roll is an ad that is placed at the very beginning of the video and mid-roll ads will show up in the middle. Both are unskippable and have a maximum time of 20 seconds. However, times are paring down somewhat, and 15 seconds is becoming the norm in terms of unskippable ads.

The cost for pre or midroll ads is what's known as CPM or cost-per-mille, meaning for every 1,000 views, you are charged. The rates, of course, vary based on a number of factors, including the ad space that you are targeting, the number of advertisers who are trying to move into the same space and the number of viewers who usually watch the types of video you are advertising in front of.

Bumper Ads:

A bumper is an extremely short ad, lasting to a maximum of 6 seconds. They are unskippable, just like pre and midroll, and they have the same fee structure. The big question would be, why use a bumper ad? Six seconds might seem very short, but the purpose of a bumper ad isn't to outright call for action. Rather that short of a time will increase what's known as ad recall lift. Ad recall lift represents how many people will remember your advertisement within a period of two days. By running small, quick bumper ads in conjunction with a larger advertising campaign, you have a greater chance of helping customers remember your ads. And if they remember your ads, they may end up deciding to check it out after a while.

Another valuable asset that bumper ads bring is the fact that they are short. Most consumers these days don't particularly enjoy ads and would much rather get through them as quickly as possible. By having these short, six second ads, you can tell your viewers about your product or promotion quickly, without having to worry about them becoming annoyed by your ad length. It's quick, effective and will help them remember you later on.

Targeted Advertising:

Once you have a general idea about the type of ad that you want to run, you'll need to make sure that you have all the data necessary for targeted advertising. Fortunately, Google's advertising systems are quite powerful, able to get your ads in front of the most relevant audience possible, provided that you have the right data for them.

The first and most important type of data to use is the right keywords. You may have a general idea of what kind of product you're going to advertise, but you'll need the right and most relevant keywords possible if you want to put your ad in front of the right people. Google has a keyword planner tool that you can use when setting up your ad. This planner will help you shape which keywords you want to target. You'll be able to see which keywords and phrases are being searched for on Google and which ones are the most relevant to your target audience. In general, you'll want to select keywords that are being searched often and by a large amount of people. This will maximize your chances of exposure, since you'll be tapping into an extremely relevant group of people.

The other types of data that you can use for YouTube Advertising involves demographics, user interests, life events and purchasing decisions. Google offers a tremendous amount of options and they are, for the most part, self-explanatory. This is one of the most important aspects of advertising, of course. The better you are able to target your audience, the more relevant your ads are and that translates to generating higher levels of conversion. Take your time and don't rush through these sections. Do everything in your power to fill out as much of these options as possible, so you have a wide, relevant audience to put your ads in front of.

Video Remarketing:

Google is able to keep track of its user viewing habits. As such, they are able to directly target people who have watched your videos or are subscribed to your channel. This practice is known as video remarketing and it is similar to Facebook's retargeting. Remarketing allows for you to create lists based on the type of viewer that you want to target. For example, if you've been doing a series about Product A, and you have 2,000 views of that product, you can create a list out of those viewers. Then, when you run your next advertisement, you can place the ad right in front of those viewers.

Remarketing is an extremely effective way to sell your products, primarily since you already know that they have demonstrated some level of interest in what you are selling. They are considered to be warm leads and as such, will most likely respond positively to your ads.

On top of that, you can also use remarketing to further hone the efficiency of the video ads after they have finished a run. If your video was displayed in front of 3,000 people, you can retarget those same 3,000 viewers later on. This is exceptionally useful when it comes to using TrueView ads, which only count a view if a consumer watches the video for thirty seconds, or until the video ends, whichever is shorter.

Since TrueView ads are opt-in, meaning customers choose to sit and watch them, they are already warmer leads than those who chose not to watch the ad at all. You can select a different, more targeted video ad to run in front of these people who have already expressed interest. This will generate a much higher return on investment.

Evaluating Analytics:

Just like with Facebook ads, running ads on YouTube is all about analytics. Once you've run a few ad campaigns, you'll have the numbers to be able to determine the efficiency of your ad campaigns. From there, you'll then have to evaluate the data and determine which ads are worth keeping, which ads are underperforming, and which ones should be reworked. Remember, when you're just starting out with advertising campaigns, you shouldn't be discouraged if you aren't seeing stellar results right out of the gate. Advertising campaigns take time to fine tune, but each time you run them, as long as you are willing to work with the data you receive, you'll be able to improve them over time. Combined with a solid video remarketing strategy, you'll be able to increase your conversion rates in no time!

CHAPTER 4

CREATING A YOUTUBE ACCOUNT

Ok, so the first step to start promoting your marketing content is by becoming an active YouTube user, and in order to become an active YouTube user you will need a YouTube account that will allow you to access every amazing feature offered by the YouTube platform.

Creating a YouTube account is as easy as easy can get, it is free and you can do it with a few clicks on your mouse. In this chapter we are going to show you how to create your own YouTube account the proper way.

Getting Started

The first step to start creating your YouTube account is to simply head to youtube.com. Now, once there you will have the option to access your YouTube account by using the sign in button but only if you have a Gmail account already.

This is because when you create a Gmail account you are signing up for the entire ecosystem of Google services, which includes popular Google platforms such as YouTube, Google Plus and Google Drive, which means that by creating a Gmail account you are also creating a YouTube account.

Enter your Gmail credentials after in order to sign in on YouTube using your Gmail account. Now you will notice that your profile image is featured in the top right corner. Click it. As you can see, you will be able to access your YouTube account from this tab, and you will have other options available such as access to your creator studios and to your YouTube account settings.

Creating A YouTube Account From Scratch

Now, you would be hard pressed to find someone who doesn't have a Gmail account nowadays, but it's possible. So in case you don't have a Google account, let's show you how you can create one from scratch, the easy way.

Start on the Google main page and click on the sign in button on the top right corner. You will be taken to a login screen asking you to enter your Gmail address, but because you don't have a Google account you will need to click on more options and then on create account.

Now you will be asked to enter your personal information to create a Google account that you can use to have your own YouTube account. Start by entering your first name and your last name. Then enter a username that will also work as your Gmail email address. Make sure that your username of choice is available. If it is not available choose one from the recommended by Google.

Now you will have to create a password and to confirm your password after you create it. Now enter your date of birth in the birthdaysection starting with the month, then the day, and then the year. Now select your gender from the gender menu below.

Lastly, enter your phone number, an up to date email address and your location, then hit the next step button to move on to the next step. A pop up window will appear instructing you to agree with Google's terms of service

Click through the terms of service document by clicking the blue scroll down button and then click on I AGREE. Now your new Google account has been created! You can access your account by clicking on the Initial Letter icon on the top right corner so you can change your profile picture by clicking on change.

Now go to YouTube so you can test your new account on the platform as well. Click on sign in and you're all set! A message that reads You are now registered with YouTube will appear to let you know that your YouTube account has been created.

Just as you saw on the previous segment, you can use the profile picture icon on the right top corner to access your account. If you want to further customize your YouTube account you can click on the YouTube settings button.

Here you will find several settings options including advanced settings, additional features, connected accounts, privacy, notifications and playback.

As you can see, creating a YouTube account is a walk in the park, and doing so will allow you to enter a world of video marketing that was just difficult to even dream up before.

The Home tab is the main tab, and in here YouTube will recommend you video content based on the type of videos that you watch or create on the platform. The trending tab features videos that are trending on YouTube at the moment, and the subscriptions tab will show you the most recent videos from the YouTube channels that you are subscribed to.

Scroll all the way down to the footer of the site and you will find some buttons that will allow you to edit some of your site preferences. Let's take a look at these buttons from left to right, starting with the language button, which allows you to switch between several languages for your user interface.

The content location menu will give you the option to select a country from which to get videos on your feed. The default content location is the country of residence that you enter when you create your account, but you can change it later using this menu if you want to view more content from different countries.

The restricted mode menu will prevent videos with inappropriate content or videos that have been tagged as such by other users from appearing on your video feed. It is set as off by default, but you can turn it on and back to off when needed.

The history button will take you to a page where you will be able to check a history of your viewed videos. Here you will be able to check your watch history as well as your search history. Clicking on the help button will display a pop up window to quickly access YouTube's help page, which is an incredible resource to check if you ever need to.

Let's lastly check the menu on the top left corner. From here you will be able to access your YouTube user options menu. First you have the home tab, which will simply take you back to the YouTube dashboard when you click it.

The my channel tab will take you to your YouTube channel. The trending tab will take you to the trending videos section, and the subscription tab will take you to your subscriptions page.

The library menu features three tabs. The first one is the historytab, which will take you to your viewed videos history so you can check which videos you have watched previously. The watch later tab will take you to a page where you can watch videos that you have marked as watch later.

This is a useful feature because it allows you to save a video so you can watch it later when you are pressed for time. You can save videos this way by hovering over a video on the video feed and clicking on the clock icon. Doing so will save your watch later video on the watch latersection.

The liked videos tab will show you a collection of your liked videos. You can like a video by clicking on the like button below a video while you are watching it. The subscriptions menu will show a list with the YouTube channels that you are subscribed to.

This menu will appear empty when your YouTube account is new because you haven't added any channel to your subscriptions up to that point. You can use the add channel and the browse channelbuttons to find channels to subscribe to, which will be added to this menu later.

You can also subscribe to a YouTube channel while you are watching a video by clicking on the subscribe button below the video. Doing so will add that channel to your subscriptions list, which you can access either through the subscription tab below the search bar or through the subscription menu on the left.

YouTube Walk Through

So you already created your YouTube account, or perhaps you had one all along without being aware about it because you never tried to sign in to YouTube while your Gmail session was open, and now you are ready to start uploading some cool marketing videos.

You've probably used YouTube before to watch videos, but YouTube goes well beyond that feature and there are lots of buttons and tabs that you might not have used yet. In this chapter we are going to show you every function available on YouTube's front page.

Let's start by taking a look at the picture icon in the top right corner to revisit the functions available there when you click it. There you have the creator studio button, which allows you to manage, check and edit your video content. Next up is the YouTube settings button, where you can manage your account settings. You can use the add account button in here to add additional YouTube accounts to this shortcut, and the sign out button will allow you to log out of YouTube.

Now this bell icon button will show you notifications on the platform, such as when your videos receive comments or likes, when you have new subscribers, and when you have set reminders to watch video events, to name a few.

The upload button will allow you to upload your video content to the YouTube platform with a few clicks on your mouse, and depending on how you plan to do your marketing this may perfectly be one of the buttons that you are going to use the most.

YouTube features a standard search bar that you can use to search video content on YouTube by using specific video titles or keywords. Below this search bar there are three video content feed tabs.

CHAPTER 5

USING YOUTUBE FOR BUSINESS PURPOSES

Reach International Audiences

YouTube is accessible by many countries around the globe. This means that not only will you be able to reach the audience in your home country, but audiences all over—leaving potential for your video to rack up hundreds of thousands of views. While this is a great benefit, there are some things that you will need to do to your video in order to avoid cultural barriers.

For example, your video may be viewed in a country where your language is not spoken. In that case, you could caption your video to reach more viewers. Additionally, you could write your title, description and tags in multiple languages as well. Facing cultural trends is another challenge. What may be of interest in your home country may not have the same appeal in another country—keep cultural trends in mind when filming your video for the best results.

Ability to Upload Short Videos

YouTube allows you to upload short videos and there is no limit on how short your video can be. This makes it easy for businesses, because the length of your video can be flexible. In most cases, shorter videos can actually hold the attention of your audience better.

Ability to Upload Longer Videos

In addition to uploading short videos, YouTube also allows you to upload long videos (15 minutes or longer). To upload long videos, you will first have to verify your account by confirming your identity through your phone. You can do this by looking under your settings and following the steps. Businesses who want to post videos of seminars, lectures, speeches etc. can benefit greatly from this feature.

Update Videos/Channel Regularly

If you're going to have a YouTube channel for your business, you should make it a general rule to upload your videos and keep your channel updated regularly. You might upload one great video and get hundreds of views on it, but after the hype is over, then what? The goal here is to keep viewers coming back to your page for fresh content. Even if you made it a goal to upload one video a month, you should definitely figure out how you're going to keep up on your channel.

Include a Call to Action on Each Video

Including a call to action on your video can encourage and inspire your viewers to take action, such as rating your video or leaving a comment. Most YouTube users do this by writing their call to action on a separate screen and editing it in at the end of the video. You can also include a call to action through an annotation. When it comes to your call of action, be creative and put it anywhere that it would fit in nicely. Some people will even put their call to action in their cover photo.

Have Personal Interactions with Viewers

YouTube is a very interactive community and you should take advantage of it to the best of your ability. Make it a goal to respond to every comment that is left on your video, even if it is just to thank that viewer for watching. By speaking directly to your viewers, it helps open the door for a developed business relationship down the line. I've found it helpful to respond to negative comments as well. Be sure to keep calm and don't attack any negative commenters. Everybody is going to run into some negative comments on YouTube once in a while. I like to handle negative comments by thanking the person for watching and asking what he or she thinks I should do better for the next time. Half the time you won't even get a reply, but it shows respect and professionalism on your part. Another idea for interacting with your viewers is to speak directly to them through your video. For example, you could say that if anybody has questions or comments he or she can leave them in a comment below and you will get back to them.

Customize the Channel to Reflect Your Business

This tip is pretty obvious, but it is important to remind yourself of its relevancy. Customize your channel to reflect your business... in other words, you probably wouldn't have tutorial videos if your business was an attorney firm, but instead you would probably have informational videos. Put yourself in your audience's shoes and ask whether the content you're sharing is helpful and relevant. Be sure to get feedback from friends and others, as their feedback will help you get better and better.

Use Creative Titles

When it comes to YouTube videos, your titles are everything. The title is one of the first things a viewer sees and often determines whether or not he or she will watch that video. For the best results, you should put some extra effort in to make sure that the titles of your video are appealing and inviting. Let's take a look at some keys for writing a good title:

Write descriptive titles. For example, if you uploaded a video of your dog doing tricks, avoid titles such as my dog or beagle playing. Titles like those don't tell you much about what's going on in the video. A better example of a good title would be Beagle Performs Amazing Tricks Video. From this title, you know that the video will be of a beagle dog doing something that you may not see every day.

Include the word video in your title. Many people search for videos in Google instead of directly in YouTube, so a typical search would be something like dog trick video and yours would likely turn up in the search results.

As always, be sure to do extensive keyword research for your title to make sure that you're using the best combination of words.

CHAPTER 6

BUILDING A YOUTUBE CHANNEL

Steven Chen, YouTube Co-founder

YouTube was originally intended as a video-dating website. Surprising, yes. In fact, according to Jawed Karim, also a YouTube co-founder (and he was actually the first one to post a video on YouTube in April 2005. His video, Me at the zoo can still be seen on YouTube), the website's original slogan was Tune in, Hook up.

Building an Audience

Building a channel has many benefits. Likewise, building an active, established community of subscribers yield better results because each time a video is posted, there is an audience ready to view and share it. There has to be an existing community that cares enough to share video content. Even YouTube says so.

In Creator Academy, YouTube's free online course for building the perfect YouTube channel, subscribers are described as the critical component to the success of a YouTube channel. They are more important than just viewers.

For starters, bad engagement is still engagement. Chances are, channel owners will not get a subscriber on the first video, so everything must be done to get that coveted subscriber. A good example is a channel with ten videos posted, but not a single subscriber. This means that the channel owner has not been doing everything to gain audience. So, how do we do it?

According to Neil Patel, co-founder of Kissmetrics (a top web analytics tool) and QuickSprout (a top business and marketing blog for tech-savvy people), there are three important aspects that channel owners must put to mind when building a target audience.

Target Audience

1. Who is my ideal customer?

Being specific about a target audience is the best. Narrowing down the list about their preferred topic, geographical location, and knowledge level can help target a more definite group of subscribers.

2. What are the goals of my target audience?

The second aspect is determining the goals of a targeted audience. Others may be trying to earn more money online, while others just want to shed weight. Others might want to start a restaurant business, while others just want to learn how to cook a mean lasagna.

It would help to think about what your target audience cares about. This should connect with a channel's product or service, though it's not necessary. For example, this eBook can be targeting 18-49 year olds, of any gender from the U.S., who want to build a better YouTube channel that can help them earn extra money. With this in mind, this eBook has been written in a tone of voice that people from that age group can understand. At the same time, the topics presented here are not fully explained in detail assuming that people in this age group already know what a video, the Internet, or a search engine is.

3. Does my audience need these kinds of videos?

Lastly, channel owners should consider whether their target audience wants videos to help them with their problems or questions. For example, it would not be advisable to create a video highlighting the tips presented in the eBook. It would be easier if this is in printed form, or simply in an eBook reader, so readers can quickly refer to the contents when needed. No need to download videos.

Meanwhile, it would be advisable to create a video promoting this eBook. Though the difference between these two scenarios is subtle, the importance can be indistinguishable. A better example is a channel for guitar tutorials. Of course, it would be better to create videos teaching how to play a guitar, so it would be easy for viewers to learn how to do it correctly. Visual examples are always helpful, but they are not appropriate for all content.

A specific target audience also makes it easier to create videos because users know what kind of videos to create. For example, creating videos that target both beginners and experts will eventually make channel owners lose part of their subscribers. Not everyone will like or understand the videos, so they will probably unsubscribe. Nobody wants that.

Creating Videos Built for a Target Audience

Meanwhile, videos should be able to help channel owners build an audience. Here are some tips how:

Prioritize the benefits that videos provide for audiences. It's more important to educate viewers first, before providing entertainment for them. Remember, YouTube is the second largest search engine today. People use it to gather information rather than seek entertainment.

Create quality videos. This means that videos should be high-quality or in high-definition with sufficient lighting and clear sound. Channel owners need to invest in video creation equipment in order to accomplish this.

Be consistent with a channel's theme, characters, and schedule of posting. This helps create brand awareness which makes audience associate a brand for a particular channel. This also includes sticking to the running length of videos. Playlists can also be created to separate quick videos and lengthy ones.

Be interesting. This is one of the major reasons why identifying a target audience is important. It's hard to keep up an audience's interest if channel owners are not aware who their target audience is and what they want. A target audience should be able to determine the interesting topics that they want in a channel.

Lastly, create collaborative videos with other channel owners. If it fits the budget, it would also be helpful to hire micro-celebrities. They are a group of people that have shown large following in social media sites, but have not been featured in TV or movies.

After identifying a target audience, and creating videos for them, it's now good to move to the next step.

CHAPTER 7

HOW SHOULD I INTEGRATE MY YOUTUBE STRATEGIES WITH OTHER SOCIAL NETWORKS?

YouTube has done a tremendous job integrating with other social media networks, and it's definitely something that you want to leverage. At the time of this writing, YouTube integrate directly with GooglePlus, Twitter, and Facebook and has great options for linking to social media on your One Channel Page. This list of options will probably change in the future, but the concepts below are true no matter what the list may hold.

It is important to note that (at the time of writing at least) Facebook can only integrate with your personal Facebook account, and not your corporate Facebook page. So the integration there is something that you'll want to examine further to decide if Facebook integration will be strategic (or distracting) for you.

Google Plus

You'll note in this book that I'm not a big fan of Google Plus. I think its impact and usefulness is greatly overstated and I don't see myself changing my mind anytime soon. The integration remains sloppy, and hard to work through, despite the millions of dollars they have thrown at it.

I do need to point out, however, that this does not mean you should ignore it in your YouTube Strategies. Google needs Google Plus to know what's important and the automatic integration of YouTube with Google Plus only means that Google will now send you more of the best possible traffic.

Action Items

What are the action items?

First, simply tie in what social networks make sense. Obviously, since GooglePlus and Twitter integrate automatically, those two are an easy decision. As a bonus tip - consider creating a Twitter

account for every YouTube channel you have.

Facebook, at this point in time however, only functions with personal account integration. In most cases, when you're using YouTube for marketing purposes, integrating with your personal account won't make sense for your business. YouTube and Facebook will probably solve this fairly soon, so keep looking into this one.

On your OneChannel, YouTube lets you link to a 4 social networks. Pick the 4 social networks that you use the most (and where you audience tends to be), not the ones you think are the most important. For example, if you have no audience on Pinterest, despite what you may hear about how popular it is, don't worry about linking to it.

YouTube is social. Making sure that everything is integrated for whatever automatic promotion YouTube might offer is an obvious strategic first step. Linking to the social accounts that you frequent the most will give you audience a better understanding of where they can find you - and give these networks the attention they deserve.

Summary

YouTube has done an incredible job integrating with other social media sites: at this point in time, GooglePlus, Twitter, and Facebook have automatic promotional elements that should be obviously integrated from day one. Your OneChannel page offers 4 links to whatever social networks you choose. Pick the ones that are smartest and most strategic for you.

Action Items

1. Tie in the social media accounts that make sense for you and

your business.

2. Go through the painful process of integrating your channel with GooglePlus; it's automatic, and creates seamless integration (and brings traffic you wouldn't have gotten otherwise) - even if your audience doesn't use it on a regular basis.

3. Create a Twitter account for your YouTube Channel if you don't already have one.

4. You can only integrate Facebook via a personal account, so at this point in time, know that this option may or may not be optimal for your business.

CHAPTER 8

HOW INCOME IS GENERATED FROM YOUTUBE

Everybody is aware that ads bring the money in YouTube, but there's more to it than just that. The job is never done by simply uploading a video.

The first thing to know about YouTube is that it's a brand of Google. Amazingly, this corporate giant owns a number of other popular brands in the internet such as Blogger, and is in partnership with vital ones like AdSense. Those who already have experience with these two will easily grasp how the video site works, and it always starts with opening a Gmail account.

Get a Gmail Account

Having a personal Gmail account is necessary because it's the gateway to Google's other products. Once you have an account, there wouldn't be a need to create separate accounts in Google+, YouTube, Google Play, and more.

Despite already having an existing Gmail account, it's still recommended to create a new one. This new account should be under the name, brand or title that will contribute to the personality of the YouTube channel. For example, if the videos to be uploaded are tutorials on how make Damascus knives, the name of the channel should be relevant to it, like The Damascus Knife Expert.

Keep in mind that the name in the Gmail account will be used in all of Google's other products. Therefore, if an existing email is for business and personal conversations, it wouldn't be ideal to change it to The Damascus Knife Expert just to suit the YouTube channel.

Setup a YouTube Channel: Creating a YouTube Personality

Personalizing the channel to suit the contents to be uploaded is the next thing to do. This, however, does not mean playing with themes and tweaking the aesthetics of the page. Adding keywords and checking the settings of the channel is necessary to maximize its contents visibility. Under the Advanced Settings of the Channel section, type in relevant words and tags. These will help make the channel more visible to people searching for similar contents. Following the example above, suggested keywords would be 'knives', 'Damascus', 'Damascus steel', 'knife making tutorial', and such.

Upload Content: Aiming for Subscribers

What's needed in every income generating YouTube account are subscribers and to get subscribers, it is crucial to upload videos regularly. Contents should also be consistent or related to each other.

Using the same example above, specifically aiming to produce knife making tutorials can be limiting. To keep videos flowing in the channel, deviating from the how-to and featuring other knife-related stuff can further attract subscribers. These other videos can feature makers of pop-culture related swords and blades, or documentaries of how Damascus steel is made.

Gain Traffic: Increasing Views

Before subscribers are fished, video contents need to be watched, and out of a hundred or a thousand views, expect to gain only one or two subscribers. They are the ones who will actively share the video in other online communities, such as Facebook, Twitter, forums and blogs.

The internet is the only place on earth where traffic is appreciated, and advertisers will pay to get a small space or time from anything viral. The more people who view the video, the more exposuretheir ads would have.

Another technique to keep audience engagement alive is to religiously answer comments. This active interaction will make people curious enough to find out more about you. Of course, this positive response will lead to more followers, and higher patronage means increased interest from possible business partners.

Earn from Videos

Money does not automatically come upon uploading a video. Some channel owners do not want ads littering their videos and page, that's why YouTube made it an option. When freshly adding a content, it will be in the default non-monetizing setting. If it's purpose is to receive passive income, users must check the Monetize with ads box under the Monetization tab.

Take note that by allowing YouTube to place ads on the video, the user acknowledges that it contains no copyrighted material.

Setup Google AdSense

This is the official partner of Google in ad placements. People looking to earn passive income from YouTube is required to create an account with AdSense. Minimum age to sign up is eighteen years old because users will be prompted to share sensitive information such as PayPal, or bank accounts and valid mailing addresses. These are to verify the identity of a person, and of course, to receive payment.

AdSense pays for clicks and views per ad. Of course, rate of the latter is lower. More views also increase the chances of people clicking on ads, and this results to higher passive income; hence, the importance of traffic.

Monitor Analytics

All of this will, of course, need marketing knowledge and strategies. Although many think it's just about selling stuff, it's actually not. Marketing utilizes statistics and relevant data to better know the market, and in turn, improve selling (or in this case, engaging) strategies.

This is also why YouTube included an Analytics tab. Users can monitor how contents are being received by their target audience. Some of the information it displays are ad performance (number of clicks and views), views, demographics, engagements (comments, shares, and likes), and estimated minutes watched.

Novices in creating video content can actually use this information to improve production elements (video length, visual presentation, entertainment value) or marketing strategies (proper targeting of audiences).

As discussed before, earning passive income from YouTube isn't as simple as uploading cat videos. The steps above should all be adhered to maximize efforts and earnings. Passive income, after all, is about upping every chance to attract the right audience.

CHAPTER 9

SEO FOR YOUTUBE

The act of posting your videos and remaining engaged with them are the two first steps to driving traffic to your YouTube channel. Without videos, there would be nothing for people to watch and without your interaction, they wouldn't stick around and continue coming back. Therefore, after a few months, you should start to see your channel receive more and more views. Continue regularly putting out more and more content. In addition, stay active and engaged with your viewers. Beyond that, there are a few more things you can do to drive traffic to your channel.

Remember that YouTube is the second largest search engine in the world. That means that your videos are most likely going to be found through people searching for them either on a traditional search engine or directly on YouTube. That means that you need to make sure your videos come up higher in the search results than similar videos posted by other people. It is a competition and you need to win. You need to elevate your videos and make them stand out because even if you have the best video in the world but it doesn't come up in search results then no one will watch it.

Thumbnail Images

In order to get people to watch your videos, you need to make sure they have good Search Engine Optimization or SEO. In addition, you need to have a good thumbnail image that shows people exactly what the video is about. Remember, a picture is worth a thousand words and, in this case, a good picture will likely be the difference between receiving views and not receiving them. After all, if there are two videos and one has an interesting thumbnail while the other is a random image of a segment in the video, which one would you choose?

Despite the saying, people do indeed judge a book by its cover. The same is true with YouTube videos. Therefore, it is essential that you have a good thumbnail image. That means that you are probably going to have to create one yourself and upload a custom thumbnail instead of using the YouTube generated images. Don't worry; it isn't very difficult. Often times you can search Google for images to use and then put them together in Photoshop or another photo editing program.

It is also a good idea to place some words on your thumbnail so people can instantly see what the video is about. The key phrase here is some words not a lot of words. Try to keep the words to a minimum and make sure they are large enough to read. People like images because images represent so much more than words and they are a lot easier to see and remember especially in a thumbnail. Thumbnails are very small so, when creating yours, remember that less is more.

Another trick you can do to help people recognize your videos and further brand your channel is to add a banner on each of your thumbnails. This will really help when your videos appear off of YouTube, like on a search engine or on social media. Adding a banner is pretty simple and can be done in many photo-editing programs. In addition, they make your videos look very professional and significantly help to increase your brand recognition.

Keywords

YouTube works exactly like a search engine by allowing viewers to search for content and then showing them videos that match their search terms. That means your videos have to be tagged and keyworded to match the search terms. Now, this may mean that your video information may not sound like it flows or may not even make sense. But don't worry because it will make sense to the search engine.

For example, if you want to know how to use Photoshop then you probably aren't going to type in a long sentence asking your question about Photoshop. Instead, you are most likely going to type in a sentence fragment or maybe even a couple of word phrases! The same is true for everyone else. People don't like to type because they are lazy. People want all the information instantly and they are not going to take the time to type out grammatically correct sentences when they are looking for something. You know this is true. After all, how many people do you know that use shorthand when sending text messages and emails?

That means you need to get up on the latest lingo and Internet abbreviations. You need to make sure your videos have the proper tags and keywords that people are going to be typing into the search bar. Don't be afraid to use the abbreviations. Remember, you are targeting 18 to 49-year-olds. Those are the people who are most often on YouTube. Therefore, they are your target audience and they are the exact people who type their queries in the search bar.

Therefore, if you have a video with great before and after images of a project or a photo you edited in Photoshop, instead of typing that entire thing out in the tag section. You will type as many variations of those words as you can think of. You may type things like Gr8, B4, Grate, et cetera. The reason is because people don't worry about spelling when they search. They know that the search engine will automatically correct the spelling and suggest results based on what they meant. Therefore, when tagging your video, use search terms so that your video will come out on top, no matter how people search for it.

That being said, you don't want to tag your videos with hundreds of tags. Doing so will only harm you because it will make your video too broad. You need to hone in and be specific. Try to limit your videos to 20 tags or less. In addition, make sure they are all directly related to your video content. This will help YouTube suggest your video to other people who have viewed related videos, which will ultimately help your channel in a significant way.

Title and Description

In addition to having a great thumbnail image and several keywords, you also need to have a captivating title and a good description. Your title is going to help entice people to click on your video and watch it. It will work hand in hand with your thumbnail image to capture interest and spark curiosity. Therefore, make sure you have a captivating title that will tell viewers exactly what they are going to watch. People like to know what is coming next. They don't want to be surprised and they definitely don't want to be disappointed.

When writing your title try to write it in keyword segments. However, unlike in the tag section, you are going to spell thing properly and make it look nice. Your title is something that needs to be appealing. Remember, people judge books by the cover so if the title looks bad then they are going to pass right on to the next one. The same is true with your video. People are going to decide based on your thumbnail and then your title whether or not they want to watch your video. Although on YouTube you will always have a thumbnail, in some search engines your thumbnail will not display. That means it is up to your title to draw them in. Therefore, make sure it is nice.

Your title and thumbnail must work together to draw people to your video.

Therefore, write your title in two or three different search phrases that tell exactly what the video is about. It is a good idea to use dividers between the phrases so that people can easily read them without having to strain their eyes. Things like dashes – or vertical bars | will work nicely. In addition, try to place your brand at the end of your title so that people will know your videos even when the thumbnail isn't present. This is mostly for off YouTube promotion like when your title is hyperlinked on another site or on social media.

Channel Details

The final thing you need to do to help your SEO is to make sure you fill out all of your channel details. This includes making sure your channel name is relevant to the type of content you are posting. In addition, make sure to add your channel keywords and other details in the settings area. Fill out your profile and add any appropriate links to your channel page, including all of your social media links. In addition, select a good profile image and a cover image that depicts the nature of your channel.

It is also important for you to take the time to add some related channels in your sidebar and, if you are able, create a video trailer for your channel. In addition, try to create playlists and video selections for people to browse when on your channel. Place these lists and videos on your channel page by adding as many sections as you want below your cover image and trailer. You may have to switch from the default YouTube channel display settings to a custom display so that you will be able to edit this information as you please.

Another thing that many YouTube channels often overlook is the Google Plus profile. You'll notice that YouTube uses your Google Plus name for your YouTube channel name unless you specifically tell it not to do so. YouTube and Google are intertwined. That means whatever is on your Google Plus profile will work to help your YouTube channel and vice versa. Therefore, make sure you take the time to completely and accurately fill out your Google Plus profile even if you never use Google Plus.

CHAPTER 10

TYPES OF VIDEO CONTENTS

Before jumping on the bandwagon and producing videos to upload on YouTube, it is important to know what contents attract traffic and how they are presented. Cat videos are awesome, but earning three figures from it is also a long shot. At the same time, overcomplicated productions may only cost more than what it is actually worth.

As mentioned before, higher views mean higher passive income; therefore, the video needs to attract a wider demographic. To achieve this, its information and entertainment value needs to be carefully measured and balanced.

To make brainstorming less strenuous, you can use the following as reference. This will also serve as the initial step in creating videos for passive income.

Tutorial Videos

Also known as how-to videos, these are basically among the easiest to produce. Everyone is an expert of something, and experience and knowledge are the only requirements for it. This can be a tutorial of any skill. Some of the most popular videos are demonstrations of:

- The use of software and programs

- Craft making and various constructions

- Repairs

- Hobbies (i.e. playing an instrument, gardening, and such)

- Sharing self-developed techniques and secrets can assure high views. In fact, these are what people look for in tutorials.

Notes:

- Determine if the demonstration is for beginners, intermediates, or experts. This can affect the scope of interested viewers, and thus the amount of passive income. Understand that introductory tutorials always have a wider audience, because the video addresses the problem of everyone who doesn't have the know-how in the most basic level. In contrast, expert level how-to's will always be limited to the number of people who already have advanced knowledge on the skill.

- Fewer minutes are always more appreciated in how-to videos. People look for straightforward and concise answers to their problems. Spending time on answering unimportant questions like who, when, where and why will only drive the audience away.

Explanation Videos or Documentaries

Think NatGeo, History Channel and Discovery when considering this type of video. It's not the cinematography that matters, however, but the questions being answered. Apart from the how, it should explain the what, when, where, who and why. The information presented should also be backed up by studies and statistics for increased viability.

These videos aren't limited to dragging subjects as well. There are YouTuber geniuses who regularly come up with simple but attention-catching topics. They focus on answering or explaining little facts, like why Americans are circumcised, or where the best vintage cars are located. Darker subjects also continue to captivate the curiosity of audience, like Illuminati secrets and alien conspiracies.

Notes:

- First of all, adequate knowledge and background on a chosen topic is needed. Being careless in presenting information can only lead to a damaged reputation.

- Ideal video length is fifteen to twenty minutes for simple and fun topics, whereas more serious ones may require hours. This video is given bigger time allowances because every question has to be answered. Its objective is to leave the audience with solid information on the subject, and should never be left with more questions.

Interviews

This is best done with a renowned personality, or someone with firsthand experience of an intriguing event. Depending on the topic or formality of the interview, these can be done via Skype Call or Google Hangouts. It is, however, always better conducted face to face, and in an animated environment.

Again, topics don't have to be serious. Some trending interviews only have a single question, but was asked to several people. For example, random women were asked what they find attractive in a guy. These interviews were compiled and uploaded as a single video.

Notes:

- Conclusions should always end the video. In the example above, for instance, the top five qualities mentioned by the women should be enumerated then added with closing remarks.

- Unless the topic is truly intriguing and the interview engaging, it should always be limited to ten minutes max.

- If the interviewee is not a celebrity, never expect it to gain a hundred thousand views. Numbers are even worse if the subject is niched, like an interview with a sword smith for example.

Interactive Videos

YouTube's developers enabled uploaders to place annotations or captions where links can be inserted; therefore, if a video needs to be linked to a website or another video, the URL, or a button containing the link, can flash or appear as the audience watch. Despite the existence of other video sites, this is only doable in YouTube.

With a touch of creativity, some YouTubers managed to produce quizzes. For example, a single video upload will hold a question, and end with multiple choice answers. Audiences can click on an answer, which will then take them to another video that opens either a second question if the answer is correct, or a clickable try again note to restart the game.

Apart from quizzes, making story consequence games is also possible. Videos will present a story, then at the end, viewers can select what ending they want it to have. This can lead to another upload showing the conclusion, or one that opens another sequence of events and set of possible endings.

The interaction initiated by these videos will spark and maintain interest and whenever it's worth spending time with, it's also worth sharing with friends. Despite greater efforts in producing one, the possibility of getting a hundred thousand views isn't farfetched.

Notes:

- Interactive videos can be in any length. As long as its entertainment value exceeds expectations, it can be longer, or in this case, more complicated.

- Creativity will always define a video from the rest; therefore, even if the link to be placed is for only a simple website, it is still advisable to make an effort to create a button for it.

Vlogs

Otherwise known as video blogs, the contents of these can basically be about anything and everything. Furthermore, not much research is needed because personal opinions will weigh more. These can be:

- Reviews for movies, books, games, and products

- Personal perspective on budding issues

- Travel experiences

- Random blurb

- Basically, whatever can be written down in blog can be said in a vlog. There's no need for complicated productions. People can literally just place a webcam before themselves then talk. Despite the simplicity, vlogs are very popular, and views can reach up to millions.

Notes:

- The more sensational the topic is, the more it will attract viewers - the legalization of same sex marriage, for example. Downside of this, however, is that it's prone to receiving negative comments from other users. But then again, the more negativity, the more likely it is to become viral.

- Aiming for a wider audience means steering away from niched subjects. Topics should be something everybody can relate to. This is why reactions on politics, entertainment industry, and blockbuster movies are always opted for.

- The shorter the video, the better. Just like in blogs, people prefer reading fewer blocks of text. The same is expected in vlogs. Once the main point has been stated, it's time to conclude the video.

Participation or Let's Play Videos

This is similar with a vlog, only that opinions are narrated over something. For example, gamers could record their game, then as they play, they speak out their commentary. Apart from production differences, what sets participation videos from vlogs is how it doesn't always have to focus on opinions. In fact, what the audience look for in this are reactions.

Some of the most popular participation videos are horror games where the players' faces are recorded.

- Again, something that everyone can relate to is preferable and though this is more popular among games, this video is also applicable on MV's or sensitive movies and books (i.e. Fifty Shades of Grey). One of the fast rising channels today is Fine Brothers Entertainment. They presented interesting settings like kids react to old computers, or teens react to 90's internet, and the reaction they get from guests are something between noteworthy, adorable and funny.

- These are often given longer times, depending on what would be reacted on. Some games, for example, last for hours, and the audience will watch it from start to finish. Creative uploaders, on the other hand, cut the video to pieces and only combine scenes with relevant reactions or narration.

Stunts, Dares and Pranks

As the name suggests, the focus of these videos are on entertainment. There's no need for it to be instilled with information because people will solely watch it for amusement.

Stunts can range from skateboard tricks and cycling dares, to cliff jumps and skydives. What will bring views in are 1) impressive and unique techniques, or 2) breathtaking and dangerous environments.

As for pranks, crazier is better. This, however, will also mean more complications in the production. Playing tricks on roommates is good, but taking it in public will definitely bring the house down.

Perhaps, the easiest to produce among the three are dares. These can be as simple as eating a spoonful of cinnamon, or dressing up like Nicki Minaj and walking in public.

Note:

- These videos have the least limitations. It can last for mere seconds or extend to twenty minutes, and people will love them all the same. As long as awesomeness is in every frame, it would make it impossible for the audience to click close.

- These are more suitable for travelers and stunt devils. Forcing oneself to perform something he's not capable of doing could only result to injuries; therefore, if going places and doing things are a regular thing, investing on a GoPro wouldn't be a bad idea. It could even bridge passion and passive income

- The limitation should be in the type of stunt, dare or prank to perform. These are not far from injuries, and doing it for the sake of uploading a video on YouTube is never worth the possible damage.

Few of the videos enumerated above will require great effort in recording and editing. That's why when choosing a type of video, always consider your own availability, money and ability.

CHAPTER 11

TYPE OF YOUTUBE VIDEOS

Before you say "Action" and actually start filming, first you need to determine what the type of your video will be. There are eight types of videos that YouTube marketers usually create:

Customer Testimonials

Customer testimonials are something that every successful brand should film at some point and upload to their YouTube channel. They are short interview-like videos where content customers are filmed to express their satisfaction with the product/service, share their positive experience with others, as well as recommend the brand to anyone who is considering their products or services.

Explainer Videos

Explainer videos are also called tutorial videos or how-to videos and their main purpose, as the name suggests, is to explain to customers how to use a particular product or service. They are also a very detailed and thoughtful way to explain some more complex customer support questions.

On-Demand Demonstration Videos

Demonstration videos are usually short videos filmed with the purpose to briefly demonstrate the use of a particular product or service, as well as to reveal its benefits to potential customers.

Case Studies and Project Reviews

Whether it is the case studies of a successful campaign or the 5-star reviews of a certain product, the purpose of these videos is to recap the positive results and share them with the world in order to turn potential customers into buyers.

Thought Leader Interviews

These videos are quality interview with experts of your niche with the sole purpose of increasing the credibility of your brand.

Video Blogs

Video blogs or usually called vlogs are frequently posted videos (on a daily or weekly basis), documenting some events. Video blogs are popular among the YouTube marketers because they are a great way to get people to visit your website. By summarizing a certain blog post and uploading the video to your YouTube channel, you also give your customers multiple options in which they can absorb your content.

YouTube Live

YouTube Live is a feature that allows you to broadcast live to your subscribers. This amazing feature is of extreme value for your marketing strategy because it allows you to connect with your audience live, and lets them engage in real-time discussions.

Event Videos

Event videos are those videos that show some experience of a conference, auction, or some other event, and are a great way to share the positive reaction of the present crowd to your online viewers.

The Script of Your Videos

Now that you've chosen the type of your video, it is time to carefully craft its script. Before you start filming, there are a couple of steps that you need to take care of in order to ensure that the video will provide value.

The Goal

Before you turn your idea into reality, you need to determine first what that idea should accomplish. What is the goal of your video? What are you trying to achieve by uploading it to your channel? Do you want to increase the number of subscribers? Enhance your brand's awareness? Drive more traffic to your website?

Of course, you want all those things, but the key to making a successful video that will be watched, is a singular goal. Make each video with a single goal in mind. This will help you stay focused and prevent tackling different things at one time, which is the best marketing practice there is.

Create the Story

Now for the creative part. After determining your goal, it is time to wake up your imagination and craft a good story for your video. This should serve as a blueprint and an outline that will be followed during the shooting process. A good video storyboard should include:

- A frame for each scene

- A short description for each of the scenes

- The lines for each of the scenes

- Camera directions and details for the shooting (for instance, wide shots, tight shots, etc.)

The Extra Elements

If you are planning to include some additional multimedia elements in your videos such as slides or graphics, then you should plan for them in advance. Make sure that the extra content will be placed without any errors and add them to your storyboard.

The Length of the Video

How long will your video be? This is an important factor in the video making process so make sure to determine this as early as possible. Videos under 2 minutes have the highest degree of audience engagement on YouTube, so keep that in mind when deciding on how long it will take for you to deliver the key message.

The Filming Location

Depending on the type and concept of your video, you may need one, two or several filming locations. Finding the perfect shooting spot can be tricky, so you might want to involve your friends and family to help you out with this one. Whatever you choose, remember that for some locations you may need a shooting permit, so take care of this one beforehand to avoid being sued.

Before shooting, visit each of the locations to determine how to adjust the scenery, take care of the lighting, pay attention to the ambient sounds, etc.

Shooting a High-Quality Video

Unless you are a very successful company and can afford to pay a fancy filming crew to take care of the video making process for you, chances are, you will need some pro tips that will help you make high-quality videos that will be watchable. Whether you are using your smartphone or a semi-professional camera for recording, the tips below will help you populate your channel with professional content:

A Tripod Is a Must. The first impression is often the most important one, especially when trying to represent your brand and promote products/services. If your video starts with a shaky camera, no one will watch it, period. When clicking on the video, people are looking to hear the story behind it, not to be distracted by the unprofessional shooting. If your shot is static, buy a decent tripod that will hold your camera steady for a professional look.

Go for Different Angles. A scene that is shot from only one angle is visually boring. To spice things up, shot each scene from a few different angles so you can edit afterward and create one appealing, expensive-like video.

More is More. Make a habit to always shoot more than you need.

That will only give you more material to choose from during the editing process and will cost nothing but a bit more time. After all, it is always easy to cut out what you don't need. Going back and re-filming is not only a hassle but sometimes impossible.

Choose the Manual Mode. I've read somewhere that real photographers use only manual mode because they get to tell the camera what they want and there are no inconvenient surprises like with automation. If your camera has that option, go for a full manual mode to get the most out of filming. That way you can easily adjust the focus and shoot a visually-appealing video.

Invest in Your Microphone. If your video includes speaking, then investing in a high-quality microphone is not an option – it is a must. You don't want to sound like you are talking to your viewers from the end of a tunnel. Even if you are using your smartphone for the video making process, you can purchase a mic that can be plugged into your device and further enhance the sound of your video.

Editing Your Video

After filming, it is time to edit the video material and create a compelling video of high quality to upload to your YouTube channel.

Editing Tools. Chances are, your OS already has some editing software that offers basic tools for editing such as correction of color, cutting clips, or adding titles. However, if you want a video with a more professional look, then spending some money on a more advanced software such as Adobe Premier CC or Final Cut Pro X, is highly recommended. If you want to keep things pretty low-budget, YouTube also offers online editing software for that purpose.

Thumbnails. As discussed earlier, video thumbnails are extremely important. The video thumbnail is what potential viewers will see in their video search results, on your YouTube channel, as well as their suggested column on their right when watching similar videos. The most successful YouTube marketers have their own custom-made thumbnails uploaded, so get creative and make one yourself.

Watermarks. Want to further encourage your viewers to hit the 'subscribe' button? Then adding a watermark is a perfect choice. Watermarks are custom-made 'subscribe' buttons that are placed on your videos with the purpose of attracting the viewer's eye and encouraging them to press conveniently and subscribe to your channel while watching your video.

If you want to add a watermark, go to 'Creator Studio'Channel' Branding'. Press 'Add a Watermark' and follow the uploading instructions.

Sound Effects. High-quality sound effects are probably the most important factor that makes the difference between a professional-shot video and an amateur one on a low budget. But you don't have to have a giant budget in order to include movie-like music. Now there are many ways to add a quality sound to your videos without draining your budget.

YouTube itself offers a variety of sound effects of high quality to choose for your videos. But if you are not so crazy about that option, then finding royalty-free music online is perhaps your best solution. There are royalty-free sounds that you can actually download for free, but if you want to add a more professional tone to your videos, then think about investing some money and download the right music for your video for a flat price. Royalty-free means that, once you pay for the download, you are free to use the music file any way you see fit, without having to make additional payments, even if your video skyrockets on YouTube.

CHAPTER 12

PUTTING TOGETHER YOUR CHANNEL

Putting together a YouTube channel is pretty simple to do. The website does a great job of walking you through it, and with a little exploring, you'll be a master.

About Section

The About section is often overlooked and not given nearly as much attention as it should on YouTube. This is mostly because when you look at somebody's profile, it's hidden in another tab, rather than right at the front, in contrast to the majority of other social media networks where it's right at the front.

While your character limit is not nearly as cramped as others, it should still be short, sweet, and simple. Treat it like you only have 100 characters, and only put the most important things there. Say what you do, your message, and your goals. You don't have to use hashtags.

At the end of your description, don't forget to add in all the links to your other social media pages, and if you have a website too. YouTube allows up to 5 links, which should be plenty. You can even customize hyperlinks up to 30 characters. You should also consider putting your business email, in case there are people who want to collaborate with you.

Your Cover and Profile Image

Keep both your profile image and your cover image simple. Your logo can act as your profile picture, and for your cover image, consider a large image with your slogan, or a small description of who you are. Keeping it simple, at least at first, is a good bet. Just make sure it's visually pleasing.

Your YouTube Trailer

YouTube actually allows you to choose a video to put right front and center on your page. One idea is to put together a trailer, clips, and things all put together to really show what your channel is about. For just starting out, just keep putting your best work up there. The absolute best video you've got, the one that best represents your company and your channel should be the first video your potential customers see.

Making your Videos

Make sure that each video is unique, but fit into the same theme as your brand. Keep a list of video ideas, and filter out the best ones. Watch other videos, of good quality who are in the same niche as you. And when you do plan to pick up a camera and start filming, a plan is never a bad thing.

It is not expensive to make a good quality YouTube video. Really, the only things you need is a camera, a tripod, and an editor. A script is also a good idea, writing down exactly what you say and what you want to cover in the video. Go into the video knowing exactly what you want to say. Also, don't forget lighting. If you can, stand in front of a window where natural daylight comes through, and film using that. If you can't, there are some great tutorials out there on how to make DIY lighting.

End the video with a call to action. Don't just end the video with a simple 'goodbye.' Make sure you tell them to subscribe, tell them where they can find the products you use in the video, and that they should comment below, telling you what they think, and like the video. Encourage constructive criticism, and ask them what they want next. This will encourage engagement.

Titles, Descriptions, and Keywords

Titles are important in YouTube. Just like how when you google a question, and websites show up with that exact question as a title, YouTube will do the same thing. The subject of your video 110% needs to be in your title.

Descriptions are also another great place to put keywords, but the best keywords should no doubt go into your titles. Descriptions should not be too long, same as your about me section. Try to stick to well-written ones, and avoid spelling and grammar errors. That's the easiest way for people to not take you professionally.

Probably the most overlooked factor in most beginners on YouTube is the thumbnail, the title page of your YouTube videos. First impressions matter! People like to say "Don't judge a book by its cover," but that is not a factor in terms of any form of social media. Make sure your thumbnail is polished, has the title in the image, and is well lit and focused. Your video thumbnail needs to stand out, and looking nice and polished is a good way to do that.

Promotion

Like stated above, you should be promoting your channel across all social media. If YouTube is going to become a staple in your marketing campaign, this is essential. Take full advantage of that share button, and make sure to let your followers know when you're posting a new video. YouTube doesn't really work as a stand-alone, as something that you use all by itself. It works much better as a companion to something else.

But, as more and more platforms work to add video streaming and content into their platforms, like Instagram with IGTV and Facebook with their video content, it might be used less and less in this way. Just something to keep in mind.

Some Basic Tips

If you really plan on using YouTube to grow, it's going to take some dedication and hard work. YouTube is entirely video content, which can take a considerable amount of more time than other platforms. Remember this before you decide that it's the best fit.

1. The best time to post content is between 12 PM and 4 PM on weekdays, and 9 AM - 11 AM. You can schedule videos to become public at these times if you don't want to think

about that.

2. Constantly promote your videos on other platforms. Tweet about them. Talk about them in your Instagram story, or put a small clip in it as a taste. Make a post on Facebook describing them. Really chat it up.

3. Post at least 5 to 10 videos before you do this. This will make it out to be like you really know what you're doing, and show dedication.

4. Be consistent with content. You should always have certain times you post, like every Wednesday at 2 PM for example. If you really want your channel to grow, posting good quality content on a regular schedule has a lot more possibilities than occasionally posting a video on a random schedule and every eight months.

5. Choose content you can make on the regular. If you're making videos that take 2 months to make, you're not going to get much growth. Create a formula where you can easily put together at least one video a week.

6. Promote at the end of your video. Talk up your channel, ask them to subscribe and engage with the video by liking or commenting. Put some thought into where the person watching would want to go after watching this video, and recommend one of your own.

Types of Videos

Tutorials: Have a product? Show them how to use it, or set it up. If your service is offering a service, show them how it can effect their lives!

Q & A: If you have questions that are always asked, answer them in a video. Make this your featured video if it just answers the basics.

Listicles: Basically, just think "Top Tens." Like "Top 10 ways to Use Your Product" or "5 Reasons Why You Need This."

Behind the Scenes: this is a great way to humanize your brand and prove that you're more than just a product. You are all human, you all work hard, and you all enjoy what you do. Show this to your fans, and you will seem more real.

Vlogs: Show them what a day working for at your business looks like. Talk to the camera, and carry it around with you all day, just going about a normal day. If you yourself don't want to do this, do it with one of your employees (if you have them).

YouTube Analytics

Once you create a high-quality video and work out all your keywords, it's time to learn about YouTube Analytics. YouTube provides you with all the information to see what kind of videos are getting the most views and engagement, what kind of videos make users subscribe to, and more. You can learn a lot about your channel and what works in it.

On YouTube Analytics, you can see everything about your viewers, from how long they stay on your videos, to their demographics. It breaks down where people are watching your videos, where they're finding them, and what device they're watching them on.

Using this information, you can figure out exactly what is working, and what isn't. It's a valuable tool that should not go unnoticed. Make good use of this, and your YouTube channel will thrive.

CHAPTER 13

MARKETING TOOLS FOR YOUTUBE

Even though many social platforms such as Facebook, Twitter and Instagram have launched video content, YouTube remains to be the king. The reason behind this is the quality options that YouTube offers that beats the other platforms hands down. Making a video and then posting it on your channel are different things to making money. Do not expect to just upload and start earning the next day just because you have content running. You have to go an extra step and market your videos and make your brand known on the internet space. The following are some of the tools that will make you achieve this

YOUTUBE MARKETING FUNNEL

The main reason for creating a funnel is not to make an instant sale. You need to create a long-term relationship with your followers and then convert them into customers once they familiarize themselves with your products. When you rank your videos on the search engine, people will have an easy time finding you. Internet users can also search for particular keywords on the YouTube search and land on your content.

Once a user clicks on your video, you can include a number of ways to move them down the sales funnel. A good example is when you include a link to a blog post within the first two sentences of your description. The blog post will give the users a detailed explanation of your products and give them a chance to opt into your mailing list. You can then send useful information to the prospects and make them part of your journey. Your focus should be on educating the followers and showing them what they will miss out if they do not use your services. Once you are convinced that they understand everything, you can then pitch a sale and wait for them to convert.

HOW TO CREATE THE PERFECT YOUTUBE SALES

FUNNEL

- Create a great landing page. As earlier stated, you can put a link on the description of your video on YouTube. It is important to make the landing page impressive and pass the right message. Ensure that the headline message on the landing page matches that on your video. Potential customers need a continuation of the same message and not an introduction to a new one.

- Create a buyer persona. The motivation for making a purchase may differ from one person to the other. Some of the key factors that can help you build a buyer persona include; how they are going to use the product, why they want to buy the product and what motivates them to buy the product. You can then personalize each customer based on the above pointers.

- Engage your audience. Once your customers have landed on your sales page, you have to look for a way to keep them there. How do you ensure that they do not unsubscribe from your list? You can come up with blog posts that you send on a regular basis. You can also send tips in your niche to create a lasting relationship with your followers.

- Convert your leads. This is the final step in a sales funnel. You have to ensure that all your efforts do not go to waste. Potential customers need a simple purchasing process but also assure to them that it is secure. You can provide a one-click signing-up option that saves them time. Ensure that you use enticing 'call-to-actions such as get 50% off if you make your purchase this week'.

AUTOSUGGEST ON YOUTUBE SEARCH

- Every time you type certain keywords on YouTube, the search engine makes suggestions based on your search history. As a beginner who only owns a channel with no content, you may not appear anywhere on this search engine.

The auto-suggest can help you come up with longtail keywords that you can use to rank your site.

Let us take for instance when you type the keywords 'how to bake' on YouTube search, you are likely to get suggestions such as

- How to bake a cake for beginners

- How to bake a cake

- How to bake cookies

- How to bake without an oven

- How to bake using a jiko

- How to bake a simple cake

- How to bake chicken

- How to bake a chocolate cake

- How to bake chicken

The list is endless. It is important to note that keyword research for YouTube is somehow different from that of Google. Most of those who head to YouTube intend to learn something and that is why 'how-to' videos are the most popular. However, some of those who search on Google may be looking for sales sites. If you do decide to use a combination of blogging and YouTube, then you have to carry out different keywords searches for each.

YOUTUBE SEARCH FILTERS

You can use YouTube's inbuilt search engine to check out similar videos in your niche before you upload one. Such an approach will give a direction that you can follow to make your videos stand out and compete with the rest. The main area of interest should be the top-ranking keywords. You can only know why they rank by examining the tags, descriptions and the thumbnails. You can click the filter button and choose one option from the many available. You can pick by 'view count' to determine what makes a good video. Click on the video and go through the description and see what stands out. You can as well sort by upload date to determine how the keywords have been performing over the years.

GOOGLE PLUS

Also known as Google Explore, you can get a better understanding of the keywords that are related to your search. You can also see user-generated content based on your base term, slang that is common in the industry and recent trends that are dominating the space. You can thus form a mental picture of what is happening in the circles of your target audience. You can thus create content that is likely to be searched for after uncovering the trends in your niche. Google Plus can show you the hashtags that are generating tons of traffic in your niche.

TUBEBUDDY

This is a 3rd party software that is also essential in YouTube marketing. With this free Chrome extension, you can optimize, promote and manage every video on your channel. There are also advanced analytic tools that you can utilize on the premium versions. It is worth noting that you do not have to leave YouTube to utilize the features of TubeBuddy. Its dominant features will show on extension, you can optimize, promote and manage every video on your channel. There are also advanced analytic tools that you can utilize on the premium versions. It is worth noting that you do not have to leave YouTube to utilize the features of TubeBuddy. Its dominant features will show on your YouTube channel and allow you to manage the videos with ease.

Some of the features that make TubeBuddy an excellent marketing tool include; Opportunity Finder. As a business owner, you have to be open-minded when it comes to making sales. This tool can help you find opportunities that you can utilize outside YouTube based on your search results and performance of your channel.

Provide captions. Your video might land on an internet user who does not understand your language. Captions can help you pass the message without listening to the accompanying audio. You can also post the transcripts as blog posts on your website.

Best practice audit. We as humans are prone to errors. This feature ensures that you do not commit any mistake when uploading your video. For instance, it can check on the size of the video, dimensions of thumbnails and whether there are any broken links in the description.

Video A\B tests. The success of your channel will depend on a number of variables. Some of the most common ones include tags, thumbnails, titles, and descriptions. This feature allows you to test the areas that are pulling you down and the ones that are performing best.

CHAPTER 14

MARKETING YOUR CONTENT

All of your efforts to conceptualize, create, edit, and upload great content would be in vain if your videos don't receive enough viewer flow. This is particularly important since if 1000 people view your content every day, only about half of them would receive ads during their viewing anyway—since YouTube arbitrarily stops ads from playing on monetized videos from time to time so that users are not inundated with an onslaught of advertising which may slow down their experience, and just annoy them in general. Out of that half, only a further half of them would interact with an ad anyway—and that's stretching it—with most just closing ad banners or videos as soon as they can. Additionally, since these ads are through partnership programs between YouTube and corporations, YouTube only pays you 55% of net revenues from the advertising of recognized partner companies, and 55% of net subscription revenues (monthly views and watch time of your content). This means that you might profit from about 1/10th (on average) of the total viewership which you receive every day. And this money isn't tax-free, so you're going to further lose out on more from whatever you earn. In fact, the average earnings per 1000 views have been pegged at somewhere between $2-$5,

As I mentioned in the beginning, this is not an easy way to make money—but could serve as a handy side-income for those who wish to dedicate time and effort into a money-making hobby. If and when you manage to separate yourself from the herd of creators out there, you may be able to earn more than enough to dedicate yourself to earning full-time from YouTube, but that will require consistent, back-breaking effort.

So, the most important thing for you to make a decent earning from all your efforts is to match that with creative marketing. Now, be aware that if you direct people to your page and attempt to direct them to click on the ads and boost your earnings in any way,

YouTube and Google will take that as an infringement of their policies—so creativity in this context doesn't refer to finding ways to sneak around YouTube policies in order to generate more clicks per minute. The only thing which would benefit you would be to get your name out there and generate more interested user traffic onto your channel.

The first step in all this is rather simple—shamelessly marketing yourself on social media. Send posts on Facebook, and tweet often, in order to get more people aware of the fact that you may have content they will enjoy. Drop hints and create mystique so that you generate more interest among people who see such posts. Or else, if you've made videos which fill up some acknowledged demand in the user market—for example, fun ways to preserve electricity, or build your own furniture, or cool computer accessories, or even political or social comedy rants, or whatever else the public has been known to enjoy—directly market your content in a witty way so that people gain more faith in the perceived value of your content and brains through your marketing slogans. While shameless marketeering may require a thick skin when you're just starting off, confidence in your own work and its worth will always pay back ten-fold. And once you've made a name for yourself, it won't seem so shameless anymore, but rather add to the just evaluation which you will have perceived to have made of your own content before you became famous.

Once you've started getting subscribers, pay attention to their feedback, and tweak your work where you feel necessary—but don't let a thousand different voices drag you into indecision. A director doesn't pander to his/her audience. Instead, they show their own skills and work in the strongest light possible while doing justice to their own beliefs and methods, and leave the rest up to the audience. If every creator would listen to the voices of the mobs while indefinitely tweaking their work to please everyone in the crowd, every last video would be largely the same. Don't lose your unique voice and talent to pander to the mob. Interact with your fans and peers through Twitter, and respond when you can to show that you care about the voices of your followers. Enjoy this stage while it lasts, because it won't be so easy or even possible to do thoroughly once you've grown substantially.

Also, get a website, and use it as a blog of sorts to showcase all your videos—with any articles that you may wish to write, or other content you may wish to launch, like podcasts—and use it as your Brand Central. This will allow you to direct most followers to a concise compilation of all forms of your work, and provide forums through which you can keep a better eye on your followers' feedback than constantly scrolling through hundreds of Google+ comments. It would also provide you with a strong landing page which you could use when partnering up for paid promotional videos with corporations. If your website receives enough visitors per day, you could also enable advertising monetization on it to supplement your YouTube income.

Another marketing method is to visit other YouTubers who may be releasing content in your genre, check out their offerings, and leave a meaningful and thoughtful comment on their video pages with links leading back to your channel. If your content truly excels on its own merit, this becomes a great way to appeal to your own target demographic without having to sift through million other uninterested viewers, since it's obvious that only people who enjoy your type of content would leave comments on pages of YouTubers who create similar videos.

Furthermore, once you start making a name for yourself, you can contact other YouTubers and engage in collaborative projects where both of you would benefit from each other's viewer base. This means getting involved in videos—either personally, or through online video conferencing software such as Skype—and creating videos which would play to both your strengths in order to come up with great content.

10 SURE WAYS TO GET MORE SUBSCRIBERS

With more and more people wanting to be famous and gain money from making YouTube videos, making a unique channel that generates a lot of traffic, views and subscribers can be rather challenging.

If you are wondering how a small channel could easily increase his reach and build his audience, you have to understand that gaining 1,000 subscribers from 0 requires a lot of patience and research. Gaining a lot of views is one thing but, how can you get your viewers to subscribe? Here are 10 strategies in which you can gain more reach and subscribers:

1. Make Quality Videos

This tip might sound like its common sense to make and produce high quality videos on time to gain a decent number of loyal viewers but some often forgets it. You cannot expect a huge number of people to take interest in your channel when you are unable to create up to date, relevant entertaining or educational material, you would probably notice a decline with your views and followers. If for example, you just created your channel and want to gain 1,000 subscribers, you have to remember that creativity is key.

2. Be Consistent

Another strategy to get more subscribers is by being consistent with the style and structure of your videos. When you look at or scan through the videos of some of YouTube's famous personalities such as TheFineBros or Smosh, you would see that their success could be contributed to the fact they indeed show consistency.

3. Be mindful of Frequency vs. Quality

You have to consider a lot of factors when it comes to choosing between the quality of your videos as well as how often you should upload new material.

If for example, your channel is mostly about vlogs about your daily life, then it is much easier to edit, publish and release a new video daily. But, if the focus of your videos is more on tutorials, short stories or informational videos that require a lot more time for editing and polishing, you can upload once or twice a week.

If you really want to have a loyal audience who is excited to view your weekly releases, you have to be able to post videos on a regular basis.

4. Ask for it

The most simple way to gain subscribers is by asking them to click on the subscribe button. You can put a call to action button at the beginning, middle or end of your videos to encourage your viewers to be a follower of your channel. You can create an effective and enticing call to action

phrase by making sure that your viewers will have an idea as to how they can subscribe and why they should.

5. Put a YT widget on your blog or site

Make your channel easily accessible to your potential followers by embedding a widget of your channel to your blog site. This will cause them to be just a click away from being subscribed to your channel.

6. Respond as soon as possible

If you really want to build your channel, you have to make your followers feel that they are important. You can do this by immediately responding to their queries, suggestions, and ideas in the comment area. If you can still handle the volume of their comments, you can write your response to them one by one. On the other hand, if the volume is too high, you can just assure them through your video that you are reading their comments.

7. Cross Promote

Another strategy to gain more subscribers is by partnering with some of your friends that also have channels so that you could promote each other's channels. You can collaborate with other YouTube users so that both of you could expand your fan base and learn from each other.

8. Stay True to Your Promises

A great way to invite more subscribers and keep your previous ones is by staying true to your word. Part of this is being consistent with uploading new content every week at the same time so that your subscribers could treat your channel as something that they could look forward to every week.

9. Utilize Annotations

Annotations are the pop up balloons that you could see when a video is playing. You can use them to invite the viewer to subscribe to your channel just by clicking on the annotation. You can convince them by providing a reason in the description area as to why they should start following you.

10. Design your Channel

Your channel consists of a header, profile picture, video trailer together with all the other videos that you uploaded. Try your best to make your channel as appealing as possible because that would be how your subscribers could know more about you and your work. Again, as much as possible, if you already have your logo, or a specific trademark, be consistent with your branding.

As you can see, you can do a lot to increase your number of views and subscribers. These strategies are just some of the tricks that you could try to build up your channel and have a bigger fan base.

CHAPTER 15

LEVERAGING YOUR COMMENT SECTION

On YouTube, one of the most underrated tools that you can use to grow your page is the comment section on your videos. The comment section on your videos gives your viewers the opportunity to comment and have a conversation with you by sharing their opinions on your videos, asking questions, and commenting on the things that they enjoy most. Although you cannot actually control who is commenting on your video or how often your videos are being commented on, you can encourage the comments through some strategies directly within your videos and within your sharing techniques. In this chapter, you are going to discover why comments are so important, how you can build better relationships with your community through them, the value that comments offer you as a creator, and how you can encourage comments on your videos.

The Value of Comments on Your Videos

As with other SEO-related activities on your channel, having people regularly commenting on your videos proves to YouTube that your video is relevant because it increases the engagement ratio on your videos. When YouTube sees that you have a higher viewership rating and plenty of people commenting on your videos, it looks to them like you are posting content that is interesting and worthy of being shown to other interested searchers. The more comments you receive on your videos, the better your video looks and the better your rankings will be.

Another benefit that you gain from having people regularly commenting on your content is that you can gain additional perspectives on the content that you are creating and what people are actually interested in gaining from your channel. When people comment, they can tell you what they like, what they don't like, what their own perspectives on your content or the topic of your content are, and what they would like to see from you in the future. This is a great opportunity for you to get inspiration for future videos as well as for you to gain perspective on what your audience wants or likes and how you can begin creating more videos that cater to their interests and desires even further.

One thing that some channels are using their comment section for is the benefit of creating authority in their niche by answering the comments that are being left under their videos. If a person comments and asks for clarification, for example, you can easily respond back with the answers they are seeking in a professional, confident manner that makes it appear like you are the authority of your niche. This type of behavior teaches people to have confidence in you and your knowledge because they can clearly see that you know what you are talking about and that you are helpful if they ever need to know more about your chosen niche. The more you encourage people to comment, asking you about questions or simply organically bring in those questions by offering interesting and engaging content and making it clear that you are available to answer those questions, the better. This not only shows that you know what you are talking about, but it also proves that you are willing to answer questions that anyone may have, which can encourage other people to ask questions should they be interested in learning more.

Lastly, a great benefit of having comments on your YouTube videos is that it encourages your audience to feel a sense of community around you and your videos. When you can encourage your audience to leave comments on your videos, it creates a snowballing effect that encourages other audience members to get involved in the discussion and carry on about the topic under your video. This begins to develop a sense of community between your audience members, and it also brings you closer together with your audience as you engage in the discussion as well and show that you are a real person who is available to have a conversation. This makes a positive impression on your audience as it helps generate a stronger relationship between you and your viewers which keeps them coming back to view more of your content and engaging with your videos. This positive social experience looks incredible on your page which will not only help build your persona and your character but also your search rankings on YouTube and other search engines that populate their lists with YouTube videos, such as Google.

Encouraging Your Viewers to Leave Comments

Comments are one of those things that you cannot entirely control when people actually leave them because the comments are being left by someone other than yourself. It is important that you realize that, even though you cannot actually force anyone into leaving comments, you can certainly encourage more people to leave comments on your videos and begin building a sort of "habit" in your audience around this. To do so, you will simply need to work in a few strategies into your videos and the incentives that you offer so that people feel inspired to actually leave a comment, rather than just keep their comments and opinions to themselves.

Below are six steps that you can use to increase the number of comments that you receive on your YouTube videos.

Step 1: Ask Questions

One way that YouTubers are increasing the numbers of contents that they receive under their videos is by asking their audience questions at the end of their videos and encouraging their audience to leave the answers in the comments section. For example, "Have you tried this method yet? If so, let me know how it worked for you in the comment section below!" or "Would you like to see more content like this? Let me know below!". Simple questions like this encourage your audience to respond to your questions through the comments section which will both encourage higher engagement ratings and will give you plenty of ideas around what type of content you can create in the future.

Aside from asking questions at the end of videos, also consider asking questions throughout the videos. Doing so makes your audience members feel actively engaged in your video which will encourage them to already be thinking about what it is that they want to say to you when you ask them to leave a comment. This is a great way to start building their inner dialogue with you so that they have enough to say when it comes to commenting that they actually feel it is worth their time to leave a comment on your video.

Step 2: Be the First to Comment on Your Videos

Believe it or not, you can actually get the comments section more engaged by being the first to comment on your own videos. Think about it this way: people rarely like to be the first when it comes to something such as engaging in a video because it would be like dancing by yourself on a dance floor. While there certainly are some people who do not care about whether or not they are dancing on their own on the dance floor, there are a majority of others will not want to be the first one out but will instead wait for someone else to go first. You need to be the first one on your videos commenting so that people see that you are actually paying attention to the comments and that they will not be talking by themselves in this section.

Your first comment needs to be something helpful and engaging, not something that is going to leave people wondering why you are acting like an audience member when you are, in fact, the content creator. Comments that encourage people to leave their own comments or to find you elsewhere online is a great way to leverage your comment section. You can also leave a little snippet of additional information in this space if you want to. As long as the comment looks genuine and interesting, you can share it with your audience and encourage them to comment back with you, trusting that they are no longer the only ones commenting on your videos.

If you do not want to be commenting alone or if you need a boost in getting people to leave comments on your channel, consider asking your close family and friends to watch the video and comment with their opinions. Do not be afraid to explain to them that it is going to help you get more views, as they will want your honesty and it will help them understand the importance of both watching the video all the way to the end and then commenting. When they realize that this will help you grow your channel, many of your loved ones will be happy to oblige.

Step 3: Recreate Your Highest-Performing Content

Again, your analytics are going to offer you the best opportunity to create your highest-performing content going forward by understanding what made your previously highest-performing videos so incredible in the first place. When you track and monitor your analytics, you can see exactly what your audience likes and what they were most willing to engage with, and you can generate new videos of a similar nature to emulate your success once again.

When you are recreating your highest-performing content, make sure that you pay attention to what exactly it was that made your audience want to comment and engage in the first place and be sure to recreate those parts as well. You do not want to be doing everything exactly the same as you had in the past, but recreating your content by using similar strategies and techniques is a great opportunity to encourage the same engagement as you had received in the past.

Step 4: Use a Contest to Increase Engagement

Contests are a great way to increase your engagement no matter what platform you are considering engaging on. When you host a contest, you can encourage people to leave comments on your videos by giving them a direct incentive to comment under your video. In this case, you want to make every single person who wants to enter the contest comment underneath the video, making that comment their entry into the contest. You can get as creative as you want in using this section for your growth, so do not be afraid to think outside of the box!

It is also important that you choose to give away something that is actually going to be desired by your audience as well. Something that is not desirable will not be much of an incentive, which may leave your giveaway ineffective and unproductive. You can easily find out what your audience would like by looking into your niche and finding out what niche-related item or service people are enjoying the most and doing your best to get something similar to offer. Of course, you will not give away anything to expensive early on, but you may benefit from doing bigger giveaways over time. In the meantime, focus on choosing something favorable and then encourage your audience to leave a comment in the comment section below in order to be entered in the contest. You might have them simply say something like "I want in!" or you may ask for them to leave you with some interesting information, such as what they would do with the prize or what their most memorable memory is. These types of contests build engagement and a relationship between you and your audience which can encourage even more growth in your channel.

Step 5: Comment on Others' Videos

If you want to encourage people to comment on your own videos, you should also be commenting on other peoples' videos, too. Each time you go on YouTube and watch peoples' videos, especially those who are in the same niche as you are, spend some time commenting on their content and engaging with their videos. Make sure that your contents are genuine and thoughtful and not an obvious marketing strategy that you are using to try and get people to look at your own channel. As well, do not be tacky in using this as an opportunity to get people to your channel by using spammy comments such as "I loved this video! You should check out mine: (link)". Instead, say something like "Absolutely! I was just talking about this in my video earlier this week! I think (insert genuine opinion here)". These types of comments show that you also upload similar content, while also making it clear that you genuinely want to share and engage. When you behave in this manner, people respect it more and are more likely to engage back with you and check out your channel to see what you are all about.

Step 6: Eliminate Spam Comments as Soon as Possible

When people leave spam comments on your videos, make sure that you remove them as soon as you see them there. Regularly check in on your videos so that you can eliminate spam and keep your comments moderated and clean. This way, when people scroll through the comment section of your videos, they do not see spammy content that leaves them feeling questionable about you and your content. Seeing spam will lead to them worrying that they may experience spam themselves if they were to engage in your video, which can leave a bad taste in peoples' mouths. Instead, you want your audience to see genuine engagement and connection happening in the comment section, which leaves them wanting to engage as well.

Engaging Back with the Comments

In addition to encouraging comments on your own videos, you need to be actually engaging back with your community when they decide to engage with your content and share with you. Encouraging people to leave comments on your videos and then never taking the time to respond or engage back makes it seem like you are just using them for credibility and growth, which will actually ruin your credibility and growth in the long run. When you go through the effort of encouraging people to comment on your videos, make sure that you are commenting back to them so that they can engage in a genuine connection with you. Even if you do not have full-on conversations through your comment section, be sure to thumbs up and comment back on as many comments as you can. This engagement shows that you care about your audience enough to actually take the time out of your day to engage back with them and nurture the relationship that you are building with your audience.

Engaging back with your audience is not only going to help nurture your connection, but it will also help you build your authority, as you know. You can also use this as an opportunity to direct your audience to follow you in other areas on the net if the comments call for it. For example, if your audience member was to say something like "I love this, but I always struggle with doing it!", you could say something like "Oh! You should check out my other video on this subject, it might help break it down for you!" or "It can be so hard sometimes! You should check out my course on this subject!". This is a great way to organically direct people into other areas of your presence so that they can follow you even more and stay connected with your message online.

Creative Marketing Strategies Using the Comments Section

Your comments are not only great for SEO, engagement, and

growth, but they are also great for actually marketing to your audience in a totally different way. This means that not only are you boosting your video's visibility, but you are also increasing your ability to make money through your account by leveraging every single section of your video for marketing.

There are a few ways that you can use the comments section for marketing, including as follows:

Responding back to questions with your offers

Leaving a comment with a link to a product or service you talk about in your video

Encouraging those who are interested in learning more about your latest product to comment below, and then responding to them

Inviting people to follow you elsewhere on the net (directing them through your funnel)

CHAPTER 17

CREATING YOUR AD CAMPAIGN

Once your marketing video is completed, the next step is to create the campaign in which you will advertise your clip on YouTube. To get started, go to Google AdWords account (sign up if you don't have one) and let's create the campaign:

Type – Click on the '+ Campaign' button and choose 'Video' to choose the type of your campaign.

Name – Here, enter the name of your campaign.

Ad Format – Choose the format of your video ad. For instance, choose 'In-stream or video discovery ads'.

Budget – Set how much money you wish to spend per day. Here, you can also select the method of delivery, meaning you can choose whether to show your video ads evenly during that day (standard delivery), or you can choose to drive views quickly (accelerated delivery).

Networks – You can choose where you want your video ads to appear. You have two options:

1. YouTube Videos: These ads will play before or mid-roll videos.

2. YouTube Search: Your ad will appear on the YouTube homepage, the video search results, and listed in the related video column.

Make sure to create different campaigns for these two networks so you can measure the success separately and more effectively.

Locations – Filter the location of the users that you want the ad to be shown to, for instance, you can only choose California, United States. You also have the option to exclude some places as well.

Language, Device & Mobile Bidding – This is a great option that allows you to specify the device, mobile carrier, and operating system for a more successful targeting. You can also decrease or increase your bid if the video is shown on a mobile device.

Advanced Settings – In this section, you can set the start and end date of your campaign, limit the daily views, create a schedule for when the ad should be displayed, etc. This allows you to personalize your ad and get the most return.

Creating the Video Ad Creative – Once you name your ad group, you can also add the link to the YouTube video that you wish the ad to play for. Then, you will choose whether you wish to display the ad as an in-display or in-stream ad.

Bidding – Choose the maximum price that you want to pay for each ad view.

Targeting – Define your audience even further to ensure views from people who will want to be engaged with the ad. You can target by age, gender, location, interest, parental status, etc.

Advanced Targeting – Here, you can target your audience by relevant keywords or even websites that you want your ad to be shown.

Linking – Finally, if you haven't done it already, link your Google AdWord account to your YouTube channel, Click 'Finish' and start your campaign.

CHAPTER 18

USING ADWORDS FOR VIDEO

You can set up your YouTube video ads campaign from your AdWords account. Doing so will allow you to leverage advertising settings that are unique to the AdWords platform such as more detailed audience targeting options and pre-set marketing objectives.

To use AdWords for video you will simply have to start on your AdWords account and from there click on the "campaigns" tab. Now click on the "new campaign" button and click on the "video" option from the campaign type selection menu to use the AdWords for video feature to launch your YouTube campaigns from AdWords.

So, the first step is to create your new video campaign, so let's show you how step by step. Start by naming your new video campaign in the "campaign name" field. Now select your type of video campaign.

You will have two type of video campaigns to choose from. The "standard" type is designed to drive views, awareness and conversions with video ads running on YouTube and on other places around the web.

The "shopping" type is designed to encourage people to buy products specifically listed in your Google Merchant Center account. You can also use the "load settings from" menu to load settings from existing video campaigns.

In our case, we are going to select the "standard" video campaign type to drive people to our business website and to increase awareness about our brand.

Now over the "video ad formats" section you will have to select your new video ad format. You can use the "in-stream or video discovery ads" format to publish video ads that appear during playtime and as search results on YouTube, or you can use the "bumper ads" format to show un-skippable 6 second video ads during mid play on YouTube videos.

In our case, we are going to select the "in-stream or video discovery ads" format to show our engaging sweepstake advert on YouTube videos and on YouTube search results, but you might want to select a different format depending on how you created your video ad and on how you would like to show your adverts to viewers on the platform.

Please note that the "maximum cost per mile" option is only available if you select the "bumper ads" format. Now, over the "budget" section you will have the options to either set a "daily" budget or a fixed "campaign total".

The "daily" budget option will allow you to set up a daily amount of money towards advertising your video campaign, which means that your daily budget will be the amount of money that you will spend on a given video ad campaign on a daily basis, and the "campaign total" option will allow you to set up a lifetime budget for this campaign's run.

Our recommendation here is to select a "daily" budget and to allocate from $5 to $30 a day depending on how much you can afford to spend on a daily basis. This will allow you to test out your campaigns and to increase your daily budget amount if you are achieving your target objectives, or to pause your campaigns and optimize them if you are not seeing an adequate return on investment over your ad spend.

Click on the "campaign start and end date" display button to set up your campaign's start and end dates. It will be set by default to start as soon as it is approved and without an end date, but you can check the calendar boxes below and to use the calendar functions to schedule your video ad campaigns.

In our case, we are going to leave our new video campaign unscheduled so we can stop it on a later date on our own. You can select on the "delivery method" display button to select an ad delivery speed.

You can select "standard" to deliver your ads evenly over the course of the day or during the length of the campaign's lifetime, or you can select "accelerated" to show your ads quickly and to as many people as possible.

In the "networks" section you can select placements to show your video ads, including YouTube search results, on YouTube videos, and on "Video partners on the display network". Our recommendation here is to leave all the options selected.

Now in the "locations" section you can select where to show your video ads, either in "all countries and territories", or in your current location. You can check the "let me choose" option to select your own target locations, which is what we recommend. In our case, we are going to select some high-spending, English speaking locations where to advertise our offer.

In the "languages" section you will be able to specify the language of your potential customers, and in the "device" section you can adjust advanced device targeting settings. Lastly, you will be able to create custom ad schedules by clicking on the "ad scheduling" display button and to set up frequency caps and content exclusions by clicking on the "ad delivery" display button.

Once you have set this up simply click on "save and continue" to move on. Now it is time to create your ad and your ad group. Start by naming your new ad group in the "ad group" field. Now enter your video ad URL in the "video ad" field.

In our case, because we selected the "in-stream or video discovery ad" format, we will have the option to customize each ad format variation separately. Start by selecting "in-stream ad" if this is your case as well.

You will simply have to enter your "display URL", which is the website address that appears in your ad, and the "final URL", which is the valid URL that people will click through to go to your site. Now select the "video discovery ad" to customize your discovery ad. Start by selecting your video ad thumbnail. Then you have to customize your headline and your description lines.

Just like we advised you on the basic campaign set up video, use headlines for short copy where you include the name of your brand, your product, or service, as well as keywords that describe the use and benefits of your offer, and use the "description line 1" field to enter your website URL, and the "description line 2" field to add a call to action or an incentive.

Then on the "landing page" section select whether to make your "channel page on YouTube" or "the video's watch page on YouTube" the video ad's landing page, and then name your video ad in the "ad name" field.

In the "bidding" section you can set a fixed maximum bid according to your bidding objective. In other words, it is the highest amount that you are willing to pay for a single view or impression, depending on which one you choose as your objective. Our recommendation here is to apply an amount a little bit above the "typical" amount recommended by AdWords right beside the amount box.

Lastly, in the "targeting" section you will be able to set up your audience targeting options. Here you will be able to customize your target audience according to "demographics" and "interests".

In the "demographics" sub section you will be able to target audiences by "gender", "age", "parental status" and "household income". How you adjust these demographic settings will mostly depend on the offer that you want to promote and the message that you want to send through your video ads, so take the time to research your target audience!

Once you have made your adjustments in this subsection simply click on "done" to save your changes. Now in the "interests" sub section you will be able target "affinity audiences" for maximum reach, to target "in-market audiences" for maximum return on investment, and to target "custom affinity audiences".

You will also have the option to target audiences by "life events" such as "college graduation", "marriage" and "moving". Lastly, you will be able to use the "narrow your audience" menu to add targeting criteria to your targeting settings including specific "keywords" and "placements", as well as to target website visitors through "remarketing" and by targeting specific topics.

Once you have set up your ad groups and ads, simply click on "save ad group". Awesome! Now your new YouTube video ad campaign is up and running alongside the rest of your AdWord campaigns. Next up we will be showing you how to set up a video remarketing campaign, so tune in!

CHAPTER 19

MAKE MONEY THROUGH YOUTUBE SPONSORSHIP

We are accustomed to seeing celebrities endorse brands on commercials that play on traditional marketing platforms such as newsprints and the TV. The tables are now turning and influencers are taking center stage when it comes to marketing products from various vendors. There are hundreds if not thousands of business owners who are willing to pay and make a sponsored video on your channel. How does it feel when you get paid to do what you like? It is definitely a good idea. The reason why business owners are shifting from celebrities to influencers is that the latter has a more engaged follower base. In fact, 92% of people interviewed recently indicate that they would prefer using a product endorsed by an influencer rather than a celebrity.

By now you already have established your niche and known how to keep your followers engaged. The next step is to look for sponsors who are willing to part with their resources and make their brands known through your channel.

Prerequisites for Getting A Good YouTube Sponsorship

Observe YouTube and Community Guidelines. This social platform has some serious rules that can lead to the termination of your account if you do not head to them. You can check some of them here http://www.youtube.com/t/community_guidelines . YouTube is also very serious when it comes to copyrights. You have to ensure that you post original content on your channel or else your account will be terminated. Make sure that your potential sponsors understand this as well before you start the sponsorship. It also thus means that you have check whether the content that your sponsors send your way is original.

You have a good performance track record. No one will be willing to partner with someone who does not perform well on this platform. Some of the areas of interest include engagement rate, likes versus dislikes on the videos and the number of views. Ensure that you have some good metrics before you go looking for sponsors.

Good subscriber base. You do not go looking for sponsors when you just have 100 subscribers on your channel. The number is not good enough to convince potentials that they will get something tangible from the engagement. A good start for sponsoring might be when you have at least 10,000 subscribers.

Categorize your channel. Potential sponsors are looking for channels that have a clear path and understand their customer base. Once you categorize your niche, then work on producing content that people can share with friends and family members. Storytelling approach will always win the hearts of your viewers and also attracts clients. Potential sponsors will analyze the nature of your channel and how your videos have been performing before they make the final decision. You should be consistent to ensure that sponsors can easily identify and make their decisions without so much struggle.

Start small. When most people hear about YouTube sponsorship, all they can think about is big brands and names in the industry. It is good to think big but convincing them might not be that easy. Big brands will be looking for Youtubers with hundreds of thousands of subscribers. Start small and target the small brands that want to create a community of followers and customers. You can then move to medium-sized firms as your subscribers' list grows. You just have to trust the process and in just a matter of years, you will be working with big brands inyour region.

How To Get YouTube Sponsorships

Some brands will come looking for you if are already an established brand. If you are not lucky, you have to do the hard task of looking for sponsors. The following are some approaches when it comes to getting sponsors

CONTACT POTENTIALS

This is the most common approach where you identify potentials and propose to partner with them. The first step is to make a list of potential brands that fit your brands' followers. If your channel targets millennial generation, then you can list down brands that have millennial products.

ATTEND PRODUCT LAUNCHES AND YOUTUBE EVENTS

Big brands such as YouTube organize meets up where users can meet and discuss and deliberate on various issues. You can meet with potential sponsors on such events and create rapport for future business engagement.

INVEST IN QUALITY

When you do a great job consistently on your channel, chances are that people will start noticing your efforts. As already stated earlier, potential sponsors are not looking for celebrities but small brands with engaged followers.

JOIN FORUMS

Such platforms are very effective when it comes to matching potential sponsors with upcoming channels. Examples of forums include Neoreach and Famebit.

How To Contact Potential Sponsors

The approach you take when it comes to contacting potential sponsors will determine whether you get a deal or not. You will get replies on some proposals while others will go unanswered. The following are simple steps on how to make the best impression

INTRODUCE YOUR CHANNEL

Chances are that the potential sponsor has never heard of you. It is thus important to introduce yourself and say what you do on your channel. You have to show how your content and brand's voice complements that of the sponsors. In simple terms, you have to illustrate how the partnership will benefit the sponsor.

HIGHLIGHT NUMBERS ON YOUR CHANNEL

Even if you do not have hundreds of thousands of followers, you can still convince a brand to work with you. Some of the important areas that a brand will consider is the engagement rate, number of views against total subscribers and conversion rates as well. Analyze data on your channel and present it in a logical manner to help potential sponsors make informed decisions.

PERSONALIZE YOUR PROPOSAL FOR EVERY BRAND

You will get hundreds of templates that people use on a daily basis to send proposals to potential brands. Chances are high that your target companies get hundreds of similar proposals every month. They will thus ignore some of them because they lack creativity and a sense of direction. If you are sending proposals to tens of companies, ensure that each pitch is unique to the company you are targeting. Go a step further and seek to know the contact person of the brand you want to target. Addressing the recipient by the name will be more attractive than simply using 'Dear Sir/ Madam.

RESEARCH ON THE BRAND

Companies want to partner with people who understand their journey and demographics. You have a look into simple things like the brand's social presence to complicated things such as sales numbers and turnover. Tell the brand the sponsorship will help them meet their sales quota or even expose them to 100,000 more potential customers. Use numbers as they are the best when it comes to convincing potential clients.

SUGGEST THE SPONSORSHIP DEAL WITH THE BRAND

Some of the potential sponsors do not even know how such a deal works. You have to take them through step-by-step and convince them that the sponsorship is a worthwhile undertaking. You can also ask for suggestions on how you can make the experience more fruitful and exciting.

Types of Sponsorships You Can Host on Your Channel

ROUTINE INCLUSION

As a host, you can also mention products that for instance helps you set up a new office. You can give some emphasis on one particular product and give a link in the description. For instance, you can highlight where you shop for a comfy office chair and give a link where viewers can purchase the same. You can then go on and discuss the other essentials of a great office.

PROVIDE PRODUCT REVIEW

This is very common in the tech industry. You can always review products and get paid for it when brands are about to introduce a new product. Some brands will even give you the product for free to use and test and come up with constructive feedback that will help improve their brands. You have to be really good in your niche for you to strike such deals.

MENTION OF PRODUCTS

You can creatively mention products either in the beginning, middle or at the end of the video. You will have to cover the product in the chosen segment and deviate from the main topic of your video. Just ensure that the transition is seamless so that your followers do not feel lost.

DEDICATED INTEGRATION SERIES

A sponsor can use your platform to produce a series of videos that will promote its products. The sponsor will have more say on the content of the videos and such an arrangement can fetch higher pay than the rest. Just ensure that videos are natural and do not contain so many salesy voices and hard sells. It is very common in the tourism industry where tour companies pay trips for Youtubers and shoot clips that promote the brand.

Tips for Creating the Perfect Sponsored Video

When you are creating videos for your channel, you are the boss and you just have to consider what your viewers are looking for. But now here you are and you have to team up with a brand that offers different products from you. Some of the companies even have an organizational culture. You may become confused and not know how to make a video that suits you both. How do you strike a balance between your channel's needs and those of your sponsors? The following are simple tips on how to overcome the nightmare

- Remain authentic. Remember that people do not come to your channel because of the sponsored video. The main reason they click on your videos is that they get value and want to learn something new. You have to give your followers what they are used to and remain your true self. YouTube followers are enlightened folks and they will note that when you try to deviate from your style. Get into talks with the sponsors and agree on how to approach the production. A good sponsor will give you the freedom to come up with content without so much interference.

- Partner with brands with a similar target audience. When you are making a sponsored video, the aim is to introduce your sponsor's products to your audience. It thus makes perfect sense to select a brand that has similar demographics in terms of audience and consumer habits. For instance, if college students make the audience for your YouTube channel, it will be of no benefit when you post a sponsored video on pension schemes. You thus have to do some basic research to land at the ideal sponsor. You can even ask your potential sponsors about the kind of audience they want to reach.

- Partner with brands that you believe in. You do not have to a sponsored video just for the sake of it. The best way to earn the trust of your followers is when you use the product that you are about to promote. You do not want a situation where your followers come to lament about the shortcomings of the products you recommended on your channel. People will start leaving poor reviews on your channel and you will be viewed as a fraud. Sometimes you can turn down sponsorship deals if you believe that the product does fit your followers.

- Be creative with the placement of the Ad. What happens when you are watching TV and an Ad comes through? Most of us scroll to the next channel. This is also what happens when you are on YouTube. You always wait for the 5 minutes to lapse to watch your favorite video. People are likely to leave your video when it starts with an advert. To avoid this and keep them hooked, you have to blend your content with the Ad in a creative way. You can have the Ad in the middle of the video or at the end.

CHAPTER 20

YOUTUBE MISTAKES TO AVOID

If you will do something wrong a couple of times, a moment will come when you will learn how to do it right. The only drawback is that this may derail you. Additionally, if you are like others, you may give up before achieving your goal.

Since you are on YouTube to make money, you don't want mistakes to hold you back. Others have already been there so you can learn from their mistakes. This will help reduce the time it will take before you start making money on YouTube.

Having Unrealistic Expectations

New YouTubers have hyped up expectations of what success is like on YouTube. They believe that, if they have a good video, it will get lots of views and make a lot of money.

If you have that mindset too, you must slow down a little. Your work does not end when you finally upload your video. Actually, uploading your video marks the beginning of a new phase that needs even more work. Specifically, you will need to promote your video. And even then, don't think you will start making money right away. It takes time.

Focusing Too Much on Short Videos

Knowing what to include in your videos to make them valuable comes with experience. As a result, you may find that most of your videos will be shorter since you are just getting started. But such videos don't usually cut it.

To begin with, they do not give the viewer enough information to help him. For example, you cannot make a decent review of your brand-new phone that lasts for 1 minute. Secondly, search engines prefer longer videos in their search results. Searching "how to draw a cartoon character" in Google brought results that are longer than 3 minutes.

However, this doesn't mean you should include fluff just to make the video longer. Viewers won't be patient to stick till the end. And this will also hurt since YouTube uses the percentage of the video watched as an indicator of quality.

A research by Buffer Social has indicated that the ideal video length is 2 min 54 seconds. But that should not limit your creativity. You can make a video that is longer than 3 minutes as long as you have reasons to justify it. I have seen videos that are 1 hour long and still manage to get lots of views.

Neglecting Audio Quality

Most people can stand a bad video. But it's only a handful of them who will put up with bad audio. And this may seem confusing since we think of the image as being more important than the audio. But the truth is that audio also matters.

Like I said earlier, you must get a stand-alone mic. This will sound better than your camcorder's built-in microphone.

Additionally, you must record in a room that is not noisy. Closing the windows and doors should help eliminate most of the sounds outside. Also, you may want to use a pop filter to reduce popping sounds.

If you find it impossible to record audio as you shoot the video, then start with the video, and do the audio latter.

Being Everything

No one will want to subscribe to your channel if it has no main theme. It could be that you have videos on sports, fashion, music, tech products, make money-online tutorials, etc.

Instead, you must have a channel for every niche you want to cover. This will make it easier to reach your target audience.

Selling Too Much

Although ads can be fun to watch, the fact still remains that they suck. And the last thing viewers want is to tune into a channel only to be bombarded with lots of advertisements.

You are free to sell as much as you want, but try to keep a balance between selling and giving your customers what they want. If you don't sell too much, you will find it easy to win the loyalty of your customers. And this will help you make more money.

Editing Too Much

Excessive editing screams "amateur work." No amount of post processing will make your video great if it is bad in the first place. So, you must focus on getting a good video when shooting. This will eliminate the need for too much editing.

There is a breed of YouTubers that just can't keep their hands from the mouse. They add so many effects to the video that instead of watching it, you are left wondering if all this was necessary.

Here is a rule you should always remember – the only edit, if you know what you are doing, will enhance your video.

CONCLUSION

Thanks for downloading this book. It is my firm belief that it has provided you with all the answers to your questions.

I hope this book was able to help you to gain a better understanding of just how useful YouTube can be for enhancing and marketing your business. If you've never considered opening up a YouTube account or if you have one but just have never really used it, I hope this book has inspired you to change that and take some action!

The next step is to figure out how YouTube can benefit YOUR business. If you don't have a YouTube account yet, I highly suggest setting one up now and going back through this book, following each step on how to optimize your account. If you are already utilizing YouTube, I suggest planning out a few goals for yourself on how you will make your YouTube channel the best that it can be! A great way to start is to review your account and determine what you should change and what you should keep doing the same. I would start out by looking at some of your video analytics, as they can tell you the best story according to numbers.

Be sure to strike when the iron is hot! When you are feeling motivated, inspired and ready to take action, take out your camera and start rolling! Some of the best videos happen when inspired action takes place. It doesn't always have to be perfect; just do your best at any given moment in time. YouTube can absolutely be used to help your brand, business or product! Be sure to take the time now to utilize the top 5 strategies you have discovered from this book and make a plan to implement them. Be sure to be as enthusiastic and helpful as possible when creating your videos and great success is sure to be yours!